Date Due

VANSep85		
Brussels		

J
971
.061
Mor

Morton, D.
Years of conflict, 1911-1921.

18057

1295

VANSep85		

J
971
.061
Mor

Morton, Desmond, 1937-. 18057
   Years of conflict, 1911-1921 / Desmond Morton.
-- Toronto : Grolier, c1983.
   110 p. : ill., maps, ports. ; 27 cm. -- (Century of
Canada series)

Bibliography: p. 110.
Includes index.
02340593   ISBN: 0717218449 :

1. World War, 1914-1918 - Canada. 2. Canada -
Politics and government - 1911-1921 3. Canada -
History - 1914-1945. I. Title.

Years of CONFLICT
1911-1921

Desmond Morton

Grolier Limited
TORONTO

CENTURY OF CANADA SERIES

SERIES CONSULTANT: DESMOND MORTON

Dedicated to Marion and David,
for whom this book is written

Acknowledgements: My understanding of Borden and his time owes much to my colleague, R. Craig Brown. Like everyone who has studied Canada's role in the First World War, I am deeply indebted to Barbara Wilson of the Public Archives of Canada and the late John Swettenham of the Canadian War Museum. The book owes its existence to Ken Pearson of Grolier and it has been immeasurably improved by the hard work of Jocelyn Smyth. Like all my books, it would never have appeared without the hard work of Clara Stewart, the protection of Kathie Hill and the patience of my wife, Jan. None of them, of course, bear any responsibility for errors and injustices that have outflanked their vigilance.

Cover illustrations:

1 | 2 / 3 | 4

1. Sir Robert Borden
2. A few of the women who, during the war, took over many jobs traditionally held by men.
3. Mounted special constables trying to control crowds during the Winnipeg General strike.
4. Canadian soldier returning from the front.

Illustration credits: Public Archives of Canada, cover (1-PA27012) (3-PAC WS-117) and pages 6 (PA80019), 9, 21 (PA12761) 26 (C14952), 29 (WS-51), 34: top left (PA24363), top right (PA24366), bottom (PA24456), 37 (TC566), 44 (PA556), 58 (PA880), 67 (C241), 70 (PA8158), 71 (PA2279), 78 (PA70057), 83 (PA2045), 87: top (PA1660), bottom (PA2946), 92 (C39556), 104 (PA97131); Ontario Archives, cover (2 and 4) and pages 40, 61, 73, 95; Manitoba Archives, pages 11, 32; City of Toronto Archives, pages 13 (top and middle) 64, 98, 106; Toronto Transit Commission, page 13 (bottom); British Columbia Archives, page 16.

Canadian Cataloguing in Publication Data

Morton, Desmond, 1937-
  Years of conflict, 1911-1921

(Century of Canada series)
Includes index.
ISBN 0-7172-1844-9

1. Canada – History – 1914-1945. 2. Canada – History – 1914-1918.* 3. World War, 1914-1918 – Canada.
I. Title. II. Series.

FC555.M6   971.061   C83-098472-0
F1034.M6

1234567890   09876543

Printed and Bound in Canada

CONTENTS

MAPS

EVENTS 1911-1921

Year	Canada	The World
1911	— Conservatives win general election; Borden becomes prime minister.	— German naval build-up continues. — Franco-Russian military alliance.
1912	— Recession hits Canada. — Regulation 17 restricts use of French in Ontario schools. — Manitoba, Ontario and Quebec boundaries extended north to Hudson Bay.	— China becomes a republic. — S.S. Titanic sinks; 1595 die. — Woodrow Wilson becomes U.S. president.
1913	— Borden's Naval bill defeated by Senate. — Over 400,000 immigrants come.	— Einstein publishes general theory of relativity; Nils Bohr explains structure of atom. — Three Balkan wars.
1914	— Ontario adopts first Workmen's Compensation Act in Canada. — British declaration takes Canada to war; Canadian Expeditionary Force leaves Quebec.	— Archduke Franz Ferdinand killed at Sarajevo. Alliance system leads to First World War. — Battle of the Marne saves Paris. — 1st Battle of Ypres stops Germans. — Turkey enters war.
1915	— 8000 enemy aliens interned. — CEF enters battle at 2nd Ypres. — Biggest wheat crop to date. — Imperial Munitions Board set up in Canada.	— Germany blockades Britain, sinks *Lusitania*, launches first air raid. — British, Australians land at Gallipoli. — Italy enters war.
1916	— Women win vote in Alberta, Manitoba, Saskatchewan. — Canadian Corps reaches full strength — 4 divisions.	— Germans attack Verdun, start bloodiest battle of war. — British offensive on the Somme. — Turks capture British army at Kut-el Amara.
1917	— Federal income tax introduced. — Military Service Act (conscription) passed. — Women closely related to servicemen get federal vote. — Borden forms Union government, wins federal election. — Canadian Corps takes Vimy Ridge. — Imperial War Conference in London.	— French army mutinies. — Russians overthrow tsar; later revolution brings Lenin to power. — British launch Passchendaele offensive. Canadians end offensive by taking Passchendaele. — United States enters war.
1918	— Exemptions from conscription cancelled. — Women over 21 get federal vote. — Government takes over Canadian Northern Railway. — Influenza epidemic.	— Russia makes peace. — German offensives almost defeat allies. — Battle of Amiens turns tide; Hundred Days advance leads to 11 November armistice. — Worldwide influenza epidemic kills as many as the war.
1919	— Winnipeg General Strike. — Laurier dies; Mackenzie King becomes Liberal leader. — Farmers movement emerges as political force. — Grand Trunk Railway nationalized.	— Treaty of Versailles signed. — First air crossing of Atlantic. — Poland, Czechoslovakia, Hungary become independent. — International Labour Conference approves 8-hour day.
1920	— National Progressive Party formed. — Canadian Air Force authorized. — Borden resigns; Arthur Meighen ends coalition, becomes Conservative prime minister. — Canada participates in League of Nations.	— League of Nations Covenant takes effect. — United States rejects League, grants votes to women. — Ireland's independence struggle ends with establishment of Irish Free State.
1921	— Canada persuades Britain to end Anglo-Japanese alliance. — Liberals win federal election, Progressives place second; Mackenzie King forms minority government.	— German reparations set at $55 billion over 42 years. — Irish Free State created. — Disarmament Conference opens at Washington.

INTRODUCTION

In the years between 1911 and 1921, Canada was split as she had not been since Confederation by the issue of conscription. Two groups of honest and honourable Canadians grew, for a time, to hate each other. The residue of that hatred still shapes the country's history and attitudes.

It is easy and tempting to take one event or issue like conscription, shake free all the other issues and events and personalities that are tangled up with it and study it on its own. This sometimes seems to make the study of history more scientific. In a laboratory, for example, we can keep pressure and volume constant and see what happens when we only change the temperature.

Unfortunately, history is not really a science, though we must be as careful as scientists in making our observations. It really is true that everything matters at once. People usually have more than one reason for doing anything important, even if they can only remember one thing at a time.

Anyone who wants to understand Canada must soon realize that it is a very complex place. That is part of the excitement and challenge of living in one of the biggest countries in the world. Just when Sir Robert Borden was most concerned about finding men for the Canadians Corps in France, he also had to worry about finding money to keep Canada's munitions factories working. Two transcontinental railways, among the biggest companies in the country, were going bankrupt. The western wheat yield was failing and the supplies of coal were shrinking so fast that factories would have to close. If that was not bad enough, one of Canada's most famous generals was found to have stolen $10,000.

History cannot get at all the facts, but it does not tell the truth if it pretends that life or government is simple. This book tries to tell the story of one of the most difficult and exciting ten years in Canadian history. Much of the book is about the man who led the country through those years. Perhaps Sir Robert Borden was not Canada's greatest prime minister. He was not a man of great flair or imagination. He was, however, an honest and a sensible man. Like other, greater men, he did not always know the right path but he never consciously stepped off it.

1

SUNSHINE SKETCHES

On election night, 1911, Halifax Conservatives reserved a room at the back of their headquarters for Robert Borden. After dinner, the party's national leader arrived to find two telegraphers checking their equipment. Results would flash to them from across Canada. Borden dutifully inspected the electrical marvel. Then he thought about the campaign.

It had been a series of wild gambles. Would Canadians vote against the one thing that so many of their politicians had sought for half a century, a reciprocity treaty with the United States? And could the incredible alliance of Conservative Imperialists and Henri Bourassa's French-Canadian nationalists survive the strain of an election campaign? All that united them was a hatred of Laurier and his "tin-pot" navy. Could that be enough or would both groups be destroyed?

Robert Borden would soon know. If he was wrong, the Old Guard would get their wish. His fifteen-year career in politics, ten of them as Conversative leader, would be over. He and Laura could return to private life. Yet, as Borden thought about the hectic weeks of campaigning, he knew that no previous campaign had gone as well. In Ontario, Premier Whitney's organization was perfect. Reports from Roblin in Manitoba and McBride in British Columbia were enthusiastic. Never in his time had bankers and businessmen poured money into party coffers more lavishly.

Yet, as Borden also knew, every election was a gamble. How could Laurier lose? Reciprocity, a Canadian navy, above all the fifteen years of prosperity: would voters ever abandon the old political magician with his eloquence and that plume of silver hair?

Outside, in the big hall, Borden heard cheers and a few groans. A grim-faced A. E. Blount, his secretary, entered. Borden's own seat was safe, but the Liberals were ahead in Halifax's other seat. Would that be the trend of the evening? It would be far worse than he had feared.

Suddenly, the telegraph chattered into life. A shirt-sleeved telegrapher ripped off a strip of paper and handed it to Borden with a smile. The news was unbelievable. Outside Halifax, both of Laurier's Nova Scotia ministers, were trailing. More results came. It was clear now. The Conservatives would have half the seats in the Maritimes, more than Borden had dreamed possible.

Next, a first trickle of returns from Quebec and Ontario. In Montreal, where Laurier had been mobbed by young nationalists, the Liberals were safe. Probably the Bourassa gamble had failed. Would it cost the Tories the election? Maybe not. The Ontario returns were unbelievable. A week before, a party organizer had boasted that the Liberals would be lucky to save sixteen seats. Borden had returned a frosty smile. Now it was clear that Laurier would have a meagre thirteen of Ontario's block of eighty-six.

From the prairies, Borden could expect little. It was there that

Opposite page: A family poses somewhat self-consciously for the camera. If the man looks a little worried, so he should: he set the timer, raced for his chair and now hopes that everyone looks natural.

the demand for free trade with the United States had reached crusading pitch. Even Conservatives had nervously echoed the cry. Alberta and Saskatchewan would give all but two of their seats to Laurier but in Manitoba an upset: Premier Roblin had delivered eight of the seats, leaving only a pair of Liberals. Finally, towards dawn, word came from British Columbia: a Conservative sweep of seven seats.

Even without Quebec, Borden would be only four seats short of a majority. And of course, English-speaking Montreal and the Eastern Townships had done their duty. Now, as he studied the pencilled figures on Blount's pad, he saw that Quebec had done much more. The little Quebec villages that had lost their sons to Montreal's factories had voted against Laurier's prosperity. Laurier would have only thirty-eight seats from his own province. Of the remaining twenty-seven, how many belonged to Bourassa, how many to Borden, only time would tell.

Canada in 1911

A year after the 1911 election, Stephen Leacock published *Sunshine Sketches of a Little Town*. Mariposa might be one of a hundred little Canadian towns; in fact it was the Ontario town of Orillia, where Leacock spent his summers. The long trains of lumber that rolled south from Orillia's sawmills would have found American markets if reciprocity had dissolved the tariff barriers at the frontier. Nonetheless, Orillia voters rejected their Liberal member. So did the voters of Mariposa.

In *Sunshine Sketches*, Leacock mocked the patriotic oratory that fuelled the Conservative compaign in Missinaba county:

> Don't ask me what election it was, whether Dominion or Provincial or Imperial or Universal, for I scarcely know. . . . I only know it was a huge election and on it turned issues of the most tremendous importance, such as whether or not Mariposa should become part of the United States, and whether the flag that had waved over the school house at Tecumseh Township for ten centuries should be trampled under the hoof of an alien invader, and whether Britons should be slaves, and whether Canadians should be Britons and whether the farming class would prove themselves Canadians, and tremendous questions of that kind.

Leacock knew that oratory. As professor of economics at McGill University in Montreal, he had thrown himself into the Conservative campaign. His phrase, "a tin-pot navy," helped sink Laurier's naval policy. Yet *Sunshine Sketches*, published in 1912, helps us understand why Canadian voters rejected both Laurier and reciprocity a year before. Since 1866, free trade with the United States had been proposed as the desperate remedy for a Canada that did not believe it could manage alone. It was a confession that Sir John A. Macdonald's attempt, by railways and tariffs, to build an independent Canada had failed. Yet nothing seemed more obvious in Mariposa or Orillia in 1911 than that Canada was at last a triumphant success.

The change had begun in 1896, the year of Laurier's victory, when the world depression lifted, when the United States ran out of free land for settlers. Large numbers of American immigrants came north to what Canadian officials called "The Last Best West." Others came from Britain and eastern Canada. Clifford Sifton, Laurier's minister in charge of immigration, sent agents to the regions we now call Poland and the Ukraine to persuade more settlers to bring their farming experience to the prairies.

The result was the fastest population growth since Confederation. In 1901, Canada had 5,371,315 people; ten years later, census-takers found 7,206,643 Canadians. Saskatchewan had grown from 91,279 people to 492,432, making it the fourth largest province. Because Europe was now eager for Canadian wheat, production soared from 56 million bushels in 1901 to 231 million,

Laurier, the "plumed knight" to his Liberal followers, could draw huge crowds even in the rain. He and his fellow Liberals believed that his defeat in 1911 had been a mistake, to be corrected at the next election.

most of it from prairie farms. The best grade, No. 1 Northern, became the standard by which all wheat was judged.

A quarter-century before, Sir John A. Macdonald had predicted the prairie settlement. He had struggled to complete the Canadian Pacific Railway because he knew it would be needed to bring prairie products east. He also believed that the railway would carry products of eastern factories to prairie settlers. By adding a high tariff to the cost of imported goods, Macdonald's National Policy made sure that even costly Canadian-made products would be cheaper than British or American goods. If all Canadians paid more for clothing or farm machinery, that was a price they must bear so that Canadian workers would have jobs.

The Liberals had bitterly opposed Macdonald's National Policy. So had many farmers, since they felt little benefit from high tariffs. However, businessmen and financiers supported the policy, and when Wilfrid Laurier became prime minister, he and his party forgot their promises of free trade — at least until 1911. And Macdonald's dream came true. The wheat boom in the West gave prairie farmers the money to buy from the East. Railway boxcars brought wheat to eastern mills and returned with farm machinery, clothing, boots, stoves and anything else farm families could afford. Business and industry shared in the boom. From 1900 to 1910, Canadian textile production doubled; the iron and steel industry tripled and the value of Canadian manufacturing rose from $214,350,000 to $564,467,000. Instead of a single transcontinental railway, the CPR, Laurier was persuaded that Canada needed and could afford three separate lines. After all, he boasted in his most famous phrase, "The Twentieth century shall be the century of Canada!"

Many Canadians agreed. Old doubts and criticisms were forgotten. In booming times, huge fortunes could be made. At twenty-seven, Richard Bedford Bennett left a meagre New Brunswick law practice to go to Calgary. Within eight years, his legal work for the CPR helped make him a millionaire. His friend, Max Aitken, left for Montreal in 1902. Four years later, he was also a millionaire. By 1910, at the age of 30, he had moved to England and won a seat in the British Parliament. Another friend of Aitken and Bennett, James Dunn, switched from law to finance and discovered how to make huge profits by investing Canadian money in foreign electricity companies.

In booming times, life grew easier and more comfortable for many Canadians. In the cities, gas replaced coal and wood for cooking while electricity, the exciting new "white coal," replaced gas in lighting streets and buildings. By 1914, more than half a million telephones were in service and 75,000 cars bumped their way over city streets or ploughed the muddy, gravelled country roads. For comfort, most Canadians travelled by railway or street-

Reciprocity
For generations, Canadians had assumed that prosperity would come from a reciprocity agreement with the United States, lowering tariffs on the goods the countries traded with each other. Such an agreement had been in effect from 1854 to 1866, and Liberals and Tories had worked to revive it ever since. However, by 1911, Canada had prosperity but no reciprocity. Perhaps it was not the magic solution after all.

A bachelor who lived in the elegant Palliser Hotel, R. B. Bennett bought one of the first automobiles ever seen in Calgary. On his first attempt to drive the machine, he managed to crash into one of the only other cars in Calgary and never drove again.

car. People still behaved very formally — even good friends rarely used first names to each other — but both men and women began to dress more comfortably. Women still wore corsets and their skirts reached their ankles, but the fashionable "new woman" was expected to be active and energetic and her clothes fitted the role. For men, the high starched collar and long frock coat already looked rather old-fashioned. In a booming, prosperous Canada, people wanted to look "up to date."

Traffic accidents were common enough even before cars filled the streets. After collision with a Winnipeg street car, a horse lies dead and a wagon is badly damaged.

Social Concerns

Of course, not everyone shared the wealth. In *Sunshine Sketches*, Leacock looks at the life and foibles of judges, clergymen, a prosperous hotel-keeper and a bank clerk with a very wealthy father. The workers in Mariposa's sawmills and their families do not appear. Some of the sunshine might have disappeared behind the clouds. If Mariposa workers shared the wages and conditions com-

THE SIMMONS FAMILY

In 1912, Albert Simmons was beginning to fit into the routine of life in Toronto. He had been here for a year, having emigrated from Brighton, England. His reasons for coming were simple.

In England, Albert and two of his brothers had worked in the family construction business. As they married and started their own families, however, the business could no longer support everyone. At the same time, the Canadian government was sponsoring a massive advertising campaign for people to come to Canada to live. Canada was painted as a land of opportunity, and Albert Simmons and his brother Syd grabbed hold of the dream shared by so many emigrants from Britain and Europe.

Armed with their tradesmen's skills, Albert and Syd boarded a ship for Canada. They were realistic enough to know that dreams are sometimes nightmares, so they left their families behind, to follow once they were established. They landed at Saint John, New Brunswick. From Saint John, Albert and Syd boarded a train full of immigrants for the long trip to Toronto. There they separated from most of the other immigrants, who were heading for the free homesteads on the western Prairies.

Cheap rooming houses abounded in Toronto, and by the next day Albert and Syd were settled in reasonable comfort. Work, it turned out, was another matter—not nearly as plentiful as they had been led to believe. But Albert and Syd were lucky. Toronto was growing, and there were still jobs for men with their skills and experience. Within a week they were working for a housing contractor. After the first pay cheque, Albert proudly wrote to his wife, Maude:

> "Well, Dear, we are both still at work. Syd only stayed at his first job a week: he got 20 cents an hour. He left on Saturday and started for another man on Monday at 30 cents on hour—and is still there. I am still with my first boss and received my first pay on Saturday. Guess what I got an hour—45 cents! I had 74 hours of work for the two weeks, that is $33.60. Jolly good, eh! I expect you will wonder what I shall do with so much—I have paid $8 for 2 weeks board and $6 towards joining the Bricklayers' society. I have still $10 to pay in the next two weeks. I have paid Syd nearly $4 and I have bought some overalls and a level and several other little things, so I have not much left of this lot."

Within a year they had saved enough money to bring over their families and their young brother, Clarence.

The reunion was a joyous one, and Maude and Bertha Simmons were delighted with the big house their husbands had rented so they could all live together. It had a piano, the one extravagance they all insisted upon as the centre of their social life.

Note how a passage from this letter has become part of the text. Historians use this technique to help people from the past speak directly to the present.

Such extravagance didn't come easily. Albert's wages covered his growing family's needs, with just a little left over—and that was wisely put aside. Albert worked 12 hours a day, 5½ days a week. So there was neither much money nor much time for entertainment. Still, Maude and Albert did occasionally treat themselves to a "Moving Picture Show" (admission five cents). And on summer Saturdays, once Albert was finished work, they often gathered up the children and caught a streetcar to Toronto harbour where a steam-driven ferry boat loaded with passengers and picnic-baskets powered its way back and forth to the amusement park and beaches of Toronto Island.

Sunday was a different kind of day. Church services occupied the morning. The children spent much of the afternoon in Sunday school while the adults got together with friends. A family dinner followed perhaps by a sing-song around the piano filled the evening.

Roles were divided. Few women worked outside the home if they could afford not to. Most found cooking, shopping, washing, child-rearing full time occupations since there were not many labour-saving machines to reduce household work. It was a busy life. It was a full life. For the Simmonses, it was even becoming a good life as Albert and Syd became the owners of their own house-building business. This didn't reduce their hours of labour, but it did increase their income considerably.

Then war was declared. Although Canadians by choice, the Simmons family considered themselves part of a greater association, the British Empire. Clarence Simmons was of military age and immediately volunteered. He trained at Valcartier and then departed with the First Contingent for England and then France. Clarence took part in the attacks on Vimy Ridge, Hill 70 and Passchendaele. He burrowed and slogged through the grey mud of the Western Front. The sweaters, mitts and food parcels sent from home were welcome, but they could only momentarily distract from the horror of modern warfare.

When peace was finally declared on November 11, 1918, the Simmons family breathed a thankful sigh of relief. Clarence had survived. Then, six days later came a telegram. Clarence Simmons had been killed on November 10, just one day before the cease-fire. He was only one of the 60,000 Canadians killed in the war. Only one of the total war dead of over fourteen million. Only a number in a tragedy that seemed to defy human scale.

But Clarence Simmons was the brother of Albert and Sydney, the son of Mr. and Mrs. Simmons. To them his death had meaning, and they would mourn him for a long time.

Life went on. The country gradually returned to normal. There was a lot of labour unrest, but it did not really affect Albert and Sydney. Their business prospered, their children grew. Still, the war had changed the world and it wasn't the same as before.

In Orillia, in 1913, the Labour Gazette *reported that sirloin steak sold at 22¢/lb., eggs were 19¢ a dozen and bread was 12¢ for a 3 lb. loaf. A 6-room house rented for $15 a month if it had indoor plumbing or $12.00 with an outdoor privy. Wages ranged from $10.50 a week for a teamster to $20.00 a week for a skilled machinist or iron moulder.*

mon across Canada, they earned twelve or fifteen dollars for a sixty-hour week. They had no paid holidays, pensions, insurance for sickness or injury or even overtime. Women earned about half as much as a man and children earned even less. Since a man's wages would cover only about two-thirds of the basic costs of the average family of five, wives and children went to work as soon as they could. In crises of sickness, injury or unemployment, workers were expected to use the money they had saved "for a rainy day."

In a little town like Mariposa, families were often large enough to share the burdens. If times were hard, there might be a nearby farm where there would at least be a roof and enough to eat. In the growing cities, such help was hard to find. Cities like Montreal, Toronto and Hamilton were growing fast, with new factories and businesses. Smaller ones were shrinking. Between 1901 and 1911, Montreal almost doubled in population, reaching close to half a million people. Toronto grew almost as rapidly. Winnipeg, the gateway to the West, exploded from being an overgrown town of 25,000 at the turn of the century to become Canada's third city, with 225,000 people. To house the flood of new city dwellers, developers built palatial mansions, rows of expensive, high-ceilinged apartments and homes, and acre after acre of cheap, crowded, unventilated tenements. In Montreal's slums, the death rate among babies was worse than in the poverty-ridden Indian city of Calcutta.

The Laurier prosperity altered the lives of millions. The Ukrainian immigrant, breaking sod in Alberta, was hardly in a stranger setting than a French Canadian from remote Beauce county working under an English-speaking foreman in a Montreal factory. A few Canadians were shocked by the results — widespread drunkenness and immorality in the streets, cruelty and violence at work or in the home, and a rising toll of industrial injuries and diseases like tuberculosis. From birth, most Canadians were taught that individuals were responsible for their own fate. If Aitken or Bennett became millionaires, that was proof of their own energy and ability. If a man lost his arm in an unguarded machine, he should have known the risks of the job. Many people were delighted to apply Charles Darwin's idea of "the survival of the fittest" to their fellow humans. While public charities helped the poor and unemployed, especially in big cities, they also tried to shame their clients into helping themselves.

Both prosperity and its price — as thousands of people were torn from their roots — angered some Canadians. Farm leaders, especially in western Canada, attacked businessmen for their huge new fortunes and for creating the evils of city life. Henri Bourassa, Armand Lavergne and the *nationalistes* in Quebec echoed the criticism. Like many leading Quebec clergy, Bourassa believed that the survival of French Canada was endangered by the mass movement of people from rural parishes to the bright lights of Montreal. Conditions in Montreal's slums and in the English-owned businesses and factories fuelled their anger.

Protestants as well as Catholics worried that slum-dwellers no longer went to church. Some church people believed that banning liquor would end drunkenness and allow poor people to live on meagre wages. A few reformers, like J. S. Woodsworth and Salem Bland in Winnipeg, went further. They insisted that the churches must preach a "social gospel" of justice and reform. They found allies in a growing reform movement among Canadian women. Evidence that families were torn apart and that children suffered in the new industrial Canada led organizations like the National Council of Canadian Women to demand reforms in public health and labour legislation. When politicians ignored the pressure, women had fresh arguments to support their demand for the right to vote. Surely they needed the political power to protect women's traditional domain, the home.

In the working-class district of Montreal, 26.8 percent of all infants died within their first year.

In a man's world, a few politicians braved ridicule to support women's suffrage. A majority of men insisted that women would debase their sex by entering the political arena. Canadian women were even divided among themselves. Not until 1909 did the National Council of Canadian Women seek votes for women. Even suffrage supporters were divided in their tactics. Flora MacDonald Denison, one of the leading organizers of the Canadian Suffrage Association, resigned as president in 1911 because of charges that she sympathized with the militant methods of British women suffragists.

In the Canadian West, where the women's movement was more radical, a group of brilliant women journalists, including Nellie McClung, Cora Hind and Francis Beynon, broadened the suffrage campaign by backing labour and temperance causes. Their favourite target became Sir Rodmond Roblin, Manitoba's pompous and condescending premier. The Manitoba women dealt with Roblin by humour. In 1914 they staged a mock parliament in which men petitioned for the right to vote, only to be met by Mrs. McClung with a parody of Roblin's arguments. "Politics," she declared, "unsettle men, and unsettled men mean unsettled bills — broken furniture, and broken vows — and divorce."

Manitoba Liberals were converted, and their election, after Roblin's Tories had been tarred by corruption, would finally win the vote for Manitoba women on January 28, 1916. Other prairie provinces, where women were backed by powerful farm organizations, followed almost at once; Saskatchewan on March 14, 1916 and Alberta on April 19.

A common target for many social critics was Canadian business. While the newspapers of the day often portrayed businessmen as the heroes of Canada's new prosperity, reformers blamed

Nellie McClung, Alice Jamieson and Emily Murphy were among the leaders of the women's suffrage movement in western Canada. To celebrate the victory in Alberta, they went out and had their picture taken.

the greed and selfishness of the rich for the state of Canadian cities. Western radicals believed that politicians who broke their promises to cut tariffs had been corrupted by eastern industrialists and financiers. Temperance crusaders blamed influential brewers and distillers for the evils of liquor. Female reformers blamed factory owners for the long hours and low wages of women workers. Such conditions, they insisted, threatened the family.

Although business was under attack for some of the ugliest features of life in 1911, its leaders could argue that they were some of Canada's most effective reformers and for the best possible reason — self-interest. If Canadians knew about the Montreal slums, it was because a young businessman, Herbert Ames, had studied them in 1897. In every city of Canada, committees of businessmen had done the hard, practical work of building hospitals, orphanages and even parks and playgrounds.

While most businessmen opposed government intervention as "socialism," they learned to make a few exceptions. Ontario municipal leaders and business leaders had helped hand over the province's hydro-electricity resources to a government commission. A few years later, industrialists and union leaders agreed to establish a Workmen's Compensation Board to help workers suffering from industrial injuries. Both developments, as progressive businessmen realized, helped Ontario become a more industrial and richer province.

A fascinating example of business-led reform was the Commission of Conservation, begun in 1909. Headed by Sir Clifford Sifton (who left Laurier's government to become a millionaire), the Commission opposed electricity exports to the United States, started to clean up the polluted lakes and rivers between the two countries and supported town planning, slum clearance and protection for migratory birds.

Such reformers got little encouragement from Sir Wilfrid Laurier. The Liberal leader was charming but he had no enthusiasm for change. It was Robert Borden, the Conservative leader, who shocked even his own party by calling for an efficient civil service, nationalization of the railways and an end to corruption. In 1908, when the Conservatives again lost to Laurier, old-guard members of the party tried to get rid of Borden. With backing from Conservative provincial premiers and from younger, reform-minded businessmen, Borden clung to the leadership. He knew though that 1911 was his last chance.

Borden believed that government must become a more efficient partner with business in managing Canada. Unlike the veterans of his party, he was fed up with the pettiness of party politics. Through the long, frustrating years of opposition, he had sustained a high vision of public duty.

On election day, few Canadians had paused to wonder whether they really wanted this solemn, high principled, slightly boring Nova Scotia lawyer to be their leader. Now they would find out.

Borden in Power

On Friday, the day after the election, Borden drove out to Grand Pré to report to the guiding figure in his life, his mother. By Sunday, he was back in Ottawa to be reunited with his wife, Laura. Already the capital was thronged with Conservatives, thirsting for jobs and contracts. On Tuesday, a hundred of them insisted on loading an embarrassed Borden into an open carriage and hauling him through the streets of Ottawa. It was an annoying interruption for a man preoccupied with choosing the ministers who would shape his government.

At last, the list was made. The key job, minister of finance, went to young Thomas White, a former Liberal who, along with Clifford Sifton and others, had broken with Laurier over reciprocity. The other appointments balanced region, province and religion. The erratic Colonel Sam Hughes as minister of militia would delight Ontario Orangemen and reward a troublesome but loyal colleague. The brilliant young Arthur Meighen would have to wait his turn; an older, less able man must have Manitoba's cabinet

Voting
In the 1911 general election, 1,307,528 voters cast ballots — 664,074 for Borden's candidates, 623,554 for Liberals and 17,900 for independent, Labour or socialist candidates. Voters had to be male, British subjects and over the age of twenty-one.

seat. The weakness was Quebec. Frederick Monk, Bourassa's ally in the Conservative ranks, bitterly opposed Borden's imperial and naval policies, but he must be included. Rather than choose untested *nationalistes* from the 1911 election, Borden chose two bumbling veterans. French Canada would have voice but no influence in the government.

There was much to do. The exasperated new prime minister found himself trapped in a cabinet that spent hours daily arguing over jobs for party supporters. Every decision, even spending a few dollars, needed cabinet approval. This was the kind of government businessmen had deplored.

Still, there was progress. Investigations were launched into alleged corruption on Laurier's cherished National Transcontinental Railway, into government purchasing and into the civil service. In a decision that gave Borden special pride, the tired old boundary dispute between Ontario and Manitoba was settled at last. Roblin would lose some of his wilder claims to Ontario territory, but his province would now run all the way to the 60th parallel and be just as big as its western neighbours, Alberta and Saskatchewan. For good measure, Ontario and Quebec would run all the way to Hudson Bay and Hudson Strait.

There was more. Borden had questioned Laurier's promise of a railway from Winnipeg to Hudson Bay, but prairie farmers pleaded for it and it would go ahead. So would Conservative promises of government-owned grain elevators, as a check to the greed of private owners. For the growing number of cars, Canada had pathetically few roads. Ottawa and the provinces, insisted Borden, must co-operate to develop highways. The tariff, too, needed to be modernized. Borden and his business friends wanted it taken out of "politics," handed over to a commission of experts. All this depended on getting an efficient civil service, not just in Ottawa where a rudimentary system of exams and qualifications existed, but also outside where thousands were hired and fired with each change of government.

So much to be done and there was so much opposition — not just from Liberals, outraged at their defeat, but from fellow-Conservatives for whom Borden's view of politics as a noble calling was evidence only of his innocence.

The Naval Question

One of the two great issues of 1911 vanished swiftly. Far from being outraged at the defeat of reciprocity, President William Howard Taft was pleased. A believer in high tariffs like the new Canadian prime minister, Taft bore Canadians no ill-will for sharing his views. Officially, Canada's relations with her powerful neighbour were conducted by the British embassy, but in the host of informal American contacts, the new government found a

Patronage
The unwritten rules of political patronage dictated that a party in power could reserve jobs and contracts for its own supporters. A change of government brought mass firing and a switching of suppliers. Naturally, government employees and contractors worked hard for the party in power. The system was inefficient, unfair and often corrupt, and more and more Canadians deplored it.

warm welcome. The two countries continued plans for a celebration in 1914 of a hundred years of unbroken, if troubled, peace.

The other issue grew steadily more serious. Almost friendless among the powers of Europe, Britain had felt secure with her vast Empire and her navy. Then, Kaiser Wilhelm II had commanded that Germany develop a navy to back up Europe's most powerful army. Britain felt compelled to keep her lead. Warships grew dramatically in cost, complexity and size. In 1906 Britain's *Dreadnought* battleship, with her speed and heavy guns, instantly made every other warship obsolete. Within three years, every navy in the world was judged by the number of these leviathans it possessed. A Liberal government took power in Britain, pledged to help the sick, the poor and the elderly. Could Britain have both welfare and the world's greatest navy? Only if she taxed her wealthy and if the Empire helped. New Zealand, Australia, even the crown colonies of Malaya were willing. Laurier had delayed, compromised and been defeated. Now it was Borden's turn.

The two prime ministers were very different in their view of Britain and of an Empire in which Canada was the oldest and largest dominion. Laurier and Borden were both strong believers in Canada. Laurier loved England and admired her system of government, but before everything he was a Canadian. Robert Borden, like many Canadians of his day, Conservatives and Liberals, felt that he was British too. He wanted Canada to help Britain but he also wanted Canada to have a direct voice in the Empire's foreign policy. The two went together in his mind. To Laurier, consultation might mean dangerous commitments that could trap Canada in "the vortex of European militarism."

During the 1911 election, English-speaking voters had discussed the reciprocity issue, while in French Canada the main issue was the Canadian navy. That was a big help to Borden because he did not have to explain why the Conservatives were, in fact, completely split between the strong imperial loyalty of the majority and the opposition of French Canadian *nationalistes* to any kind of help for Britain. Now the split would be obvious.

Both wings of the Conservatives agreed that spending on Laurier's little navy should be cut off. Recruiting stopped and the new naval college was closed. The next step was harder. Other dominions and colonies had sent money to pay for Dreadnoughts; surely Canada was rich enough to pay for three of them — $35 million. In the summer of 1912, Borden went to England. He returned convinced by Winston Churchill, the British minister responsible for the Royal Navy, that the need was real. Unfortunately, Borden had no success at all in persuading the British that Canada should have a voice in setting Empire foreign policy.

There would be time for that later. In the naval race with Germany, a hard-pressed Britain needed help at once. First the Con-

Dreadnoughts
The Dreadnought *class of battleship had oil-fired turbines, whereas previous big warships were fuelled by coal. Instead of carrying a collection of big, medium and small guns, it concentrated its firepower in a few huge guns, mounted in giant turrets. It could out-run and out-shoot any ship afloat.*

Laurier's Navy
Laurier had tried to satisfy both the Conservative Imperialists and the French-Canadian nationalists by having Canada establish a navy of her own instead of sending money to pay for ships for the British Navy. A tiny fleet on each coast began in 1910 with the loan of two old British cruisers that would serve as training ships until more ships could be built in Canada. The compromise was denounced as too little by the Conservatives and as too much by Bourassa and his nationalists, who wanted no navy at all.

servative cabinet, then Parliament, debated a Naval Aid Bill. French Canadians were furious. Frederick Monk demanded a national referendum on the question. When Borden refused, he resigned. Other Quebec Conservatives were expected to follow. Had they not been elected as enemies of imperialism? They preferred to stay with the government: a furious Bourassa sneered at them as "temporary nationalists" and traitors to Quebec.

Sensing that Borden might be in trouble, Laurier and the Liberals kept arguing about the Naval Aid Bill for week after week. The Canadian Parliament had no rules for ending a debate, but Arthur Meighen invented a rule for "closure" and got the law through the House of Commons. The Senate was a different story. Filled with Liberals appointed by Laurier, the Senate defeated the Naval Aid Bill. For good measure, it defeated Borden's tariff commission and his highway programme too, defying the Conservatives to call an election.

By the summer of 1913, Robert Borden had enraged the Quebec nationalists, failed to help Britain's navy and seen some of his favourite reforms defeated. Maybe it was time for an election. There was only one problem. By then, Canada was in the worst economic depression since 1896. The Laurier boom was over.

The Borden Depression

Canada's economic troubles began long before Borden took power. As early as 1907, prices in much of the world had begun to rise. Countries looked for cheaper sources of wheat. Russia and Argentina became Canada's competitors. Britain had invested huge sums in Canada for railways, factories and businesses. Suddenly the British began keeping more money at home. Ripples spread through the Canadian economy. Factories slowed production and laid off workers. Farmers decided not to buy new machinery. More and more immigrants crowded into Canada. There seemed to be no way of stopping the flow, but now there was little or no work for them. In British Columbia, people clamoured for ·the Conservatives to keep their election promise to ban all Oriental immigrants. In the summer of 1914, the *Komagata Maru* arrived at Vancouver crowded with Sikhs from India, some of them former soldiers of the British Empire. The government forbade them to land and at last a ship from Canada's neglected navy escorted the *Komagata Maru* out of the harbour. For a moment at least the Borden government was popular in British Columbia.

Such moments were rare. Voters might not believe that governments should interfere in the economy, but Canadians had also always held politicians responsible for bad times. Like other finance ministers, Thomas White insisted that, in time, the depression would cure itself. Meanwhile, governments must cut spending to match falling revenues and do their utmost to encourage business confidence. Looking after the hungry and the unemployed

Closure

Closure allows a cabinet minister, after giving due notice, to move that the question being discussed not be considered further. Such a motion is not debatable and must be voted on at once. If it passes, any more speeches · on the subject are limited to 20 minutes and a vote must be taken by 1 A.M. (originally 2 A.M.) the following day.

Closure was borrowed from the British Parliament where it had been used to end deliberate obstruction by Irish nationalist M.P.'s.

was the responsibility of the provinces, the cities and private charities.

There were some victims of the depression that Borden's government could not ignore: the transcontinental railways.

It was very unfair. In opposition, Robert Borden had warned that the Liberal policy was disastrous. He was right, but his attacks only drove the army of promoters and lawyers and contractors who would profit from the billion-dollar project closer to the Liberals.

A sensible policy had been possible. The Grand Trunk Railway had served much of Ontario and Quebec since the 1850s. Two crafty promoters, William Mackenzie and Donald Mann, had thrown together a system of branch lines called the Canadian Northern to serve nine-tenths of the prairies. Put together, with a little help, the combined systems could connect East and West, cross the Rockies to the Pacific and rival the widely detested CPR.

That did not happen. Mackenzie and Mann insisted on their own system, and by organizing financial and political allies, they got Laurier to approve huge land grants and loan guarantees. Meanwhile, the Grand Trunk offered Laurier a proposal he could

Life for prairie settlers could mean years of poverty. Those who arrived just before the war found drought, falling prices and anything but the golden promises that drew them to Canada.

not refuse. They could build the Grand Trunk Pacific, linking Winnipeg and Prince Rupert. Meanwhile, the government itself would link Winnipeg with Quebec City, cross the St. Lawrence and link up with the Intercolonial Railway to Halifax. By crossing northern Quebec and Ontario, this "National Transcontinental" would open huge tracts for French Canadians to establish new parishes. There was no end to the political and economic gains to be made from the two new systems and, of course, there could be no end to the Laurier prosperity.

But the end *had* come. Now both railways were beating on Borden's door. He might cheerfully have sent them packing, waited for bankruptcy and taken them over as a government railway system, as he had proposed in 1907. Instead, the prime minister was deluged with warnings. Canada's reputation as a good place to invest might be ruined. The Bank of Commerce, which had supported the Conservatives in the 1911 election, might collapse. It was cunning and effective blackmail. Instead of promoting the causes he cared about, Borden had to clear up Laurier's misjudgements. He had to wring from a reluctant Conservative caucus and then from Parliament enough money to get Mackenzie and Mann through 1913. They were back again in 1914. To keep Quebec happy, the government had to pour money into the National Transcontinental and the colossal engineering work of the Quebec Bridge. Twice the span collapsed before a final success in 1917.

As if the economy and the Liberal Senate were not problems enough, Borden's fellow-Conservatives in Ontario chose the moment to drive a further wedge between French and English. After years of pressure from Protestants, joined later by Irish Catholics like Bishop Michael Fallon, the Whitney government decided to abolish most of the opportunities French-speaking Ontarians had enjoyed to educate their children in French. There were some reasonable arguments for Ontario's Regulation 17, but it was — and it was seen to be — an attack on the rights of French Canadians to preserve their language and culture as equals in Canada.

There was not much that a federal government could do about provincial education policy, and there was even less after Premier Whitney took the issue to Ontario voters in 1914 and won a sweeping victory. For Conservatives across Canada, there was not much else to cheer. In cities and towns from coast to coast, thousands looked for work. On the prairies, the 1913 crop was bad and the 1914 harvest would be even worse. It was obvious now that large areas of the "Last, Best West" should never have been opened for farming.

Bad times and the frustration of Borden's own programme brought alarming signs of turbulence. Delegates to a Social Services Conference in 1914 agreed that Canada must have a system

Maria Chapdelaine, *one of the best-selling books ever written about Canada was published in France in 1914. Its author, Louis Hémon, a young French writer who had come to Canada in 1911, had been killed by a train near Chapleau, Ontario, in 1913.*

of old age pensions, public housing in her cities and pensions for single mothers. In Toronto, voters across the city elected a socialist, Jimmy Simpson, to the Board of Control. Far away, on Vancouver Island, hundreds of soldiers were still on guard in a bitter, year-long miners' strike.

Far away, on June 28, 1914, in the drab Bosnian town of Sarajevo, a terrorist named Gavrilo Princip killed an Austrian grand duke. Another tiresome Balkan crisis had begun. Canadians did not know it but their *Sunshine Sketches* were over.

REVIEW AND DISCUSSION

Note: Many of the "Key People" who are identified in one chapter appear in others as well. Readers should keep track of the ongoing importance of these individuals.

Key People and Ideas
Explain the importance of each of the following people and ideas as they are discussed in the chapter.

Robert Borden	Reciprocity with the United States
Henri Bourassa	Macdonald's National Policy
Sir Wilfrid Laurier	National Council of Canadian Women
J. S. Woodsworth	Commission of Conservation
Nellie McClung	Naval Aid Bill
Stephen Leacock	Ontario's Regulation 17

Analysing the Issues
Answer each of the following questions, which deal with important issues raised in the chapter.

— What were the signs of growing prosperity in Canada between 1900 and 1914?
— What was the evidence that everyone did not share in this prosperity?
— What were the key issues facing Robert Borden when he came to power in 1911?
— What were the economic troubles which led to the "Borden Depression"?

Questions for Discussion
Think carefully about each of the following questions and discuss the issues they raise.

— How justified were the criticisms aimed at businessmen in the early nineteenth century? What arguments might businessmen have used to defend themselves against their critics?
— Was Robert Borden correct when he viewed politics as a "noble calling", or was this opinion in fact "evidence only of his innocence"?

2

READY, AYE, READY!

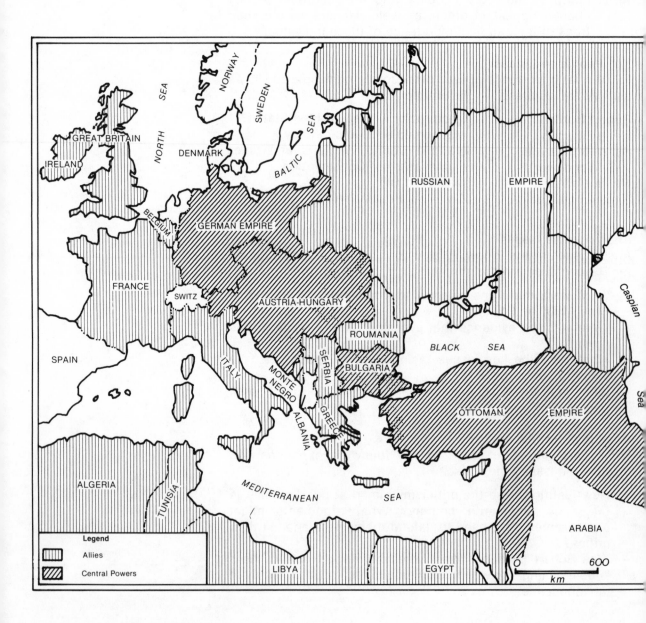

In the hot Canadian summer of 1914, the European crisis rumbled like a distant thunderstorm. Few people took the threat of war seriously. Diplomatic crises had become commonplace. Even if Europe slid into war, surely Britain's peace-minded Liberal government would keep the Empire neutral. Canadians might even profit from war contracts. The European peasant would learn, Toronto's *Saturday Night* magazine smugly predicted, that:

> . . . there are countries located on the North American continent where he will not suddenly be drafted into a conflict in which he has no interest and no heart, to be pulled and hauled about and maimed and killed.

The Coming of War

Ever since French soldiers had been humiliated by more efficient German armies in the Franco-Prussian war of 1870, France had yearned for vengeance. Weaker than the new German empire, the French had made an alliance in 1894 with the Russians. It was risky. The Russian tsar's armies were huge but inefficient and ill-equipped. Russia had other allies — weak and quarrelsome countries like Serbia. In turn, Germany made an alliance with the Austro-Hungarian Empire, a ramshackle collection of dozens of nationalities and languages, most of them eager to be independent of the eighty-four-year-old Emperor Franz-Josef and his brilliant capital of Vienna. It was Franz-Josef's grandson and heir who had been killed by the terrorist's bullets at Sarajevo. With a terrifying inevitability, Europe's alliance system clicked into place.

Since Serbian conspirators had hatched the plot at Sarajevo, the Austrians demanded that Serbia pay a heavy price. Russia, as defender of all Slavic peoples, including the Serbs, could not allow it. Austria mobilized her armies and Russia followed. On August 1, Kaiser Wilhelm II mobilized Germany's army not just against Russia but against her ally, France, as well. Too weak to defeat both of her neighbours at once, Germany planned to hold off the Russians while a complex system of roads and railways raced a huge army westwards across neutral Belgium to smash the French in a flank attack.

In theory, the British had no reason to get involved. Years before, the Germans had been Britain's natural allies; the French and Russians were the enemy. The Kaiser's decision to challenge Britain's seapower with his own high seas fleet turned the two countries into deadly enemies. Britain needed allies. That was why she had turned to her own colonies for naval help. For more powerful support, Britain had made a cautious "Entente" or understanding with the French and Russians, and British army officers met with the French to talk over what might be done if a war came. Still, there were no official commitments.

However, there was one half-forgotten treaty. In 1830, Bri-

Serbia
Serbia was a small Slavic kingdom on the southern border of the Austro-Hungarian Empire, cut off from the sea. Although Serbians were defeated and overrun during the war, the allies restored the kingdom at the end of 1918, added neighbouring territories and allowed the creation of the modern state of Yugoslavia.

The German Empire
Prussia became the heart of the German Empire proclaimed in 1870. The king of Prussia became Kaiser, or emperor, of Germany.

Sir Wilfrid Laurier addresses a recruiting rally in Montreal. Note that most of the symbols reflect Canada's British and Imperial connection, even though the crowd was made up mainly of French-speaking Quebeckers. Note, too, that Laurier speaks without benefit of a microphone.

tain, France and Prussia had all agreed to preserve the neutrality of the little kingdom of Belgium. On August 1, the Germans tore up that "scrap of paper." German guns pounded the Belgian frontier forts. A worried British government sent a warning. The Germans must withdraw by midnight, August 4, 1914, or the British Empire would declare war. The ultimatum expired unanswered.

"When Britain is at war, Canada is at war", had declared Sir Wilfrid Laurier in 1910. "There is no distinction." The news reached Ottawa at 8:55 P.M. and flashed across the country. As in the European capitals, excited crowds filled the streets. Reporters claimed that the throngs in Montreal and Quebec City were bigger and more enthusiastic than in Toronto or Vancouver. Canadians appeared united as never before. Henri Bourassa, who had narrowly escaped from Germany and who came back through wartime France, declared that the crisis might create a sacred unity of French and English Canadians. In Ottawa, Laurier promised a political truce as long as the war lasted.

On August 18, Parliament met in an emergency session. Recalling his words of 1910, Laurier drew cheers as he proclaimed, "When the call comes, our answer goes at once, and it goes in the classical language of the British answer to the call of duty, 'Ready, aye, ready!'" When W. F. O'Connor, a Halifax lawyer, took on the job of writing a law to give the government enough power to

cope with the crisis, it was a Liberal who insisted: "Make absolutely sure that you omit no power that the government may need." O'Connor's War Measures Act allowed the Cabinet to approve anything it thought necessary "for the security, defence, peace, order and welfare of Canada." No one in 1914 could have imagined how far the Act would go.

Mobilizing Canada

On July 29, a week before the declaration, a message from London had advised the Canadian government to take precautions. As Sir Robert Borden hurried back to Ottawa from a holiday, soldiers and the few remaining Canadian sailors moved to protect Halifax from surprise attack. In British Columbia, Premier McBride hurriedly purchased two submarines being built at Seattle to provide a little security for the Pacific coast. By August 2, men of the Canadian militia guarded vital bridges, canals and railway tunnels against sabotage. On August 6, Canada offered Britain a force of 25,000 men.

Canadians have always been told that they were unprepared for war in 1914. So was every country, even Germany, for the appalling struggle it now faced. Canada was probably better prepared than for any other war before or since. Under Laurier, Canada's militia had been expanded and modernized. Under Colonel Sam Hughes, military spending rose from $7 million in 1911 to $13.5 million in 1913. In 1904, 25,000 volunteers had trained; in 1913, 55,000 part-time soldiers and 44,000 members of school cadet corps went to militia camp. New artillery and equipment poured into Canada as fast as British factories could deliver them. As early as 1902, Sam Hughes had persuaded the Laurier government to produce his favourite rifle in Canada. Though the Ross rifle had serious weaknesses, Hughes forbade any criticism of the weapon.

In fact, Hughes allowed no criticism of anything he did, whether it was banning liquor from militia camps, buying Ford cars for the militia staff or taking a bevy of officers and their wives to see the British, French and Swiss manoeuvres. Hughes crisscrossed Canada in his private railway car, opening armouries and warning of imminent war with Germany. By 1914, "Drill Hall Sam" had become Robert Borden's biggest embarrassment. Even some fellow-Conservatives thought he was crazy. On August 4, Hughes suddenly looked very sane.

A former newspaperman who always gave reporters a good story, Hughes had plenty of support from the press. Militia officers were delighted to have a minister who defended and expanded the force at every opportunity. Many of them also agreed with Hughes that amateur soldiers could outfight professionals.

Since 1911, Hughes's staff officers had worked out a careful

The Ross Rifle
From the government's point of view, one big advantage of the Ross rifle was that the inventor, Sir Charles Ross, was willing to manufacture it in Canada. An excellent target rifle (it was still used by Canadian snipers in the Korean War, 1950-53) the Ross was long, heavy and easily jammed by dirt. When fired rapidly, the mechanism heated up and often seized. Obviously, it was a poor weapon for trench warfare.

plan to send a force of about 25,000 Canadians to fight "in a civilized country in a temperate climate." Now that the plan was needed, the minister cancelled it. Instead, hundreds of telegrams to militia colonels across the country summoned volunteers by the thousand. An army of workmen scurried to Valcartier, a sandy plain twenty-five kilometres from Quebec City, to lay out tents, roads and the biggest rifle range in the world. By early September, 32,000 men and 8000 horses had poured into the camp. A sweating, happy Sam Hughes, promoting cronies, damning critics and boasting of his achievements, struggled to bring order out of the chaos he had created.

Most Canadians, including the prime minister, thought it was a marvel. They had no idea that professional staff officers had plans which could have avoided confusion, allowed proper training and created a contingent that might have represented all of Canada. Thanks to Hughes, the French-Canadian volunteers disappeared into two separate battalions and there was no single unit to represent them or, for that matter, the province of Nova Scotia. When Borden gave permission for all 32,000 volunteers to go overseas, Hughes wept with gratitude; but the disorder in loading all the men, horses and equipment into thirty ships was indescribable. On October 3, when Hughes passed through the convoy on a final visit, he delivered bundles of his farewell message. "Men", it declared, "The world regards you as a marvel." Soldiers scrunched the leaflets and rained them down on the minister's launch.

"Twenty-two volunteers were chosen and, on Friday, August 14, clad in their red tunics, blue trousers and white helmets, they marched to the railway station. . . . They were supported by the Citizens' Band and the Collegiate Cadets Bugle Band. . . . It was a gala event. The women of the town presented $80 to the contingent and the Council next day presented each man with $10 and each officer with $15. The war, of course, would be over in three months."

Leslie Frost describes the departure of Orillia's contribution to the First Contingent.

"Over by Christmas"

If the untrained soldiers of Canada's First Contingent had any real worry on that October afternoon, it was that the war would be over before they arrived. For dozens of excellent reasons, experts insisted that the war could not last past Christmas. Already the death toll was appalling. National morale could not stand the strain. Neither could economies. Nations would go bankrupt under the cost of the mass armies and their modern weapons.

The truth was that few people anywhere — and least of all in Canada — had any experience of war or any concept of what it might involve. Perhaps the closest parallel to a modern war had been the American Civil War of 1861-65. Many Canadians had crossed the border to fight in that war, but by 1914 even the youngest of them would be almost eighty years old. People's ideas about war had been shaped by short conflicts in remote places. There were few photographs to bring home reality; instead, war artists portrayed fighting as a romantic business with flashing sabres and heroic charges.

Canadian soldiers would soon find out the ugly truth about war, but few people in Canada ever did. For most of the first year of fighting, they believed that the war would end soon — in an

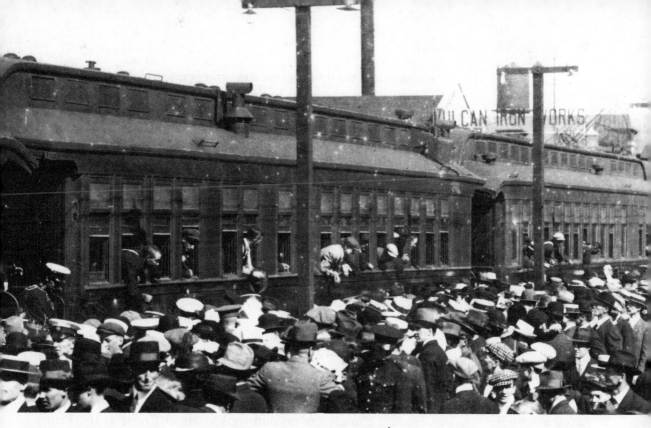

allied victory of course. Then the defeated Germans would pay back the cost of the war — already half a million dollars a day for Canada by the end of 1914. Meanwhile, only volunteers would be needed for the Canadian Expeditionary Force and married men must have their wives' permission.

Unfortunately, despite the censorship of war news and the optimistic claims of victory, the war showed no signs of ending. The German flank attack had rolled through Belgium on schedule. It had smashed into the French and British armies, only to be stopped and shoved back at the very gates of Paris. Next, the Germans had tried desperately to cut the allied armies off from the English Channel. At Ypres, in a last corner of Belgium, the battered remnants of the British army had barely held the line. By November of 1914, two opposing lines of trenches faced each other from the Swiss border to the sea. They would stay there for four more years.

Only a German victory or a compromise could ever have ended the war quickly. Now, after months of terrible sacrifices, after atrocities real and alleged, compromise was impossible and defeat unthinkable. Still, only a few people in 1914 foresaw how long and hard the war would be. Lord Kitchener, the veteran commander invited to take charge of Britain's military efforts, appalled his fellow ministers by asking for a million soldiers. Eventually, Britain would need five times as many. In Canada, Major-General Willoughby Gwatkin, chief of the militia staff, tried to hold down the size of Canada's expeditionary force. He foresaw

Men of Winnipeg's 90th Rifles, "The Little Black Devils," leave for Valcartier in August 1914. Across Canada, stations were thronged by excited crowds. Many soldiers wondered whether they would arrive before the fighting was over.

that there would never be enough volunteers. Hughes and Borden ignored his warnings. In September 1914, Henri Bourassa offered some wise advice. The government, he said, should make a clear plan "before starting or pursuing an effort that it will perhaps not be in a state to sustain until the end."

Bourassa made sense, but already he had lost any enthusiasm for the European war. Among other Canadians, passions were only beginnning to rise. It is hard for any democracy to fight a war by half-measures. Either the struggle is a crusade or it is not worth fighting. Imperialists identified with Britain and the Empire in the struggle. Others, like J. W. Dafoe, editor of the Manitoba *Free Press*, had insisted from the first that it was Canada's war. Canadians, he said, had a duty to fight for democracy and freedom against Prussian militarism. More and more people agreed.

Patriots and Pacifists

Before the war, many leading Canadians had called themselves "pacifists," or opponents of any kind of fighting. Canadian women who demanded the right to vote often argued that women would never allow wars with all their killing and destruction. Protestant church leaders had spoken about Christ as the Prince of Peace. In 1912, the Trades and Labour Congress had said that workers should go on strike if a war was declared. Some religious communities like the Mennonites and the Doukhobors had come to Canada on the promise that they would never be forced to join the army. Canadians welcomed them as excellent farmers whose opposition to war was no greater than that of many Canadians.

Almost as soon as the war began, Canadian pacifism dissolved. The religious communities did not change their minds. Centuries of persecution had tested the pacifism of Doukhobors, Quakers and Mennonites. Others had lonelier struggles. The Rev. J. S. Woodsworth, a leading Methodist, resigned from the ministry in 1917 after he had been driven from his work. Francis Beynon, who had edited the women's page of the *Grain Growers' Guide*, the biggest farmers' paper, finally moved to New York. Radical labour leaders continued their opposition, but they had to realize that their members overwhelmingly supported the war.

So did most of those who had opposed war and denounced militarism before August 1914. In a struggle against "the demon Hun", anyone who refused to join the fight was as bad as an enemy. Ministers who had preached against war now used their pulpits as recruiting platforms. Woodsworth was shocked when a leading Montreal Methodist, the Rev. C. A. Williams, used his sermon to command the young men of his congregation to join up. He was horrified when, at the end of the service, recruiting sergeants appeared at the doors of the church. Leading feminists spoke at recruiting rallies. Ontario women wore badges saying

In schools, students joined an "Arithmetic War" in which every problem solved was a German prisoner captured. When thirty prisoners were taken, the student was promoted from private, advancing to the highest rank. Essay competitions set topics such as "Soldiers at the Front" and "Why the Empire is at War."

"Knit or fight" and handed out white feathers — a symbol of cowardice — to young men in civilian clothes.

Patriots had much to do. Since soldiers could hardly support their families on a private's pay of $1.10 a day, a Canadian Patriotic Fund was organized. Within three months, $6 million was raised. Soldiers' families depended on this private charity until 1916, when the government took over. When sick and wounded soldiers began coming back from the war, the government set up a Military Hospitals Commission to create hospitals and nursing homes. Businessmen took charge of these activities. Many women worked with the Patriotic Fund, the Red Cross and a host of other organizations. A few designed their own uniforms and tried to drill like soldiers. Their effort dissolved under ridicule. Even school children collected money to buy machine guns for the army. All were expected to "do their bit." Those who did not were condemned as "slackers."

War-bred passions easily turned to hatred and intolerance. In 1914, more than 100,000 Germans and Austro-Hungarians lived in Canada. They ranged from businessmen, scientists and respected municipal officials to thousands of the unskilled workers building the transcontinental railways. From Ottawa, the Borden government pleaded for justice and restraint. It did nothing to stop the few Germans and Austrians who wanted to fight for their homeland from slipping across the border in the first weeks of the war.

Ordinary Canadians would not be so patient. Although no act of spying or sabotage was ever proved, public opinion demanded that the "enemy aliens" be fired from their jobs and locked up. By the end of 1914, Ottawa had opened the first internment camps, and within a year more than 8000 Germans and Austro-Hungarians had been confined. Many were merely unemployed workers whom municipal authorities patriotically refused to support.

Interning men of military age who belonged to an enemy power was part of the rules of war. Many Canadians, including a French-Canadian member of Parliament, were interned in Germany during the war.

Patriotism was not yet satisfied. The loyalty of 400,000 Canadians of German origin was publicly and regularly questioned. The old town of Berlin in western Ontario was threatened with a boycott until its German-speaking citizens reluctantly changed the name to Kitchener in 1916. Winnipeggers decided to eat "nips" instead of hamburgers. Symphony orchestras stopped playing the works of composers like Beethoven and Wagner, and German could no longer be taught in schools and universities, certainly not by teachers of German origin. Little boys gradually grew tired of chasing dachshunds and pelting them with stones.

Industries for War

Part of the bitterness against "enemy aliens" in the first year of the war may have been due to the continuing depression. Even by the winter of 1914-15, thousands of Canadians were still out of work. Two-thirds of the young men who had trooped to Valcartier

Recruits training in western Canada. The straw hats, known as ''cow's breakfasts,'' were part of the uniform. Note the variety of ages and uniforms. Part of unpreparedness was a lack of army clothing and equipment.

were young British immigrants, most of whom had never found a job in Canada. Many more joined a Second Contingent when it was approved in October. Western Canada sent more men than its quota because drought had destroyed much of the 1914 wheat crop. The war made the economy worse. Nervous buyers cancelled orders. Massey-Harris, the big farm machinery manufacturer, complained that thousands of its big new machines had been delivered to Europe in the spring but now there was no way to collect the money for them.

The only economic bright spot was the chance to supply Sam Hughes's soldiers and the hope that when the Canadians showed off their new boots, uniforms and farm wagons, massive war contracts would follow. Instead, after a few months in England, Canadians discovered that their boots leaked, their uniforms were cheaply made and their wagons could not carry a full load of ammunition. Canada's reputation was not helped when a crowd of shady promoters arrived in London, some of them armed with recommendations from their good friend, Colonel Sam Hughes. The British preferred to place their orders through their New York agent, the banking firm of J. Pierpont Morgan.

In Ottawa, Sir Robert Borden (he had been knighted before the war) was furious. Canada had sent soldiers and even 100,000 bags of flour. She was entitled to business. He complained of a ''very painful and even bitter feeling'' when Canadian workers went hungry while orders went to their neutral neighbours in the United States. The answer, of course, was to stop whining and start selling. Sam Hughes mustered a group of militia friends and manufacturers, called it his "Shell Committee" and soon won British orders worth $25 million. More orders followed. Trench warfare devoured immense quantities of shells and Britain's munitions industry was hopelessly overloaded.

Of course, Canada did not have a munitions industry at all beyond the rifle cartridges and a few artillery shells produced at a small government factory outside Quebec City. Hughes's Shell Committee was better at promises than performance. Very few Canadian factories had ever done precision work. Faulty shells could easily blow up guns and the men who served them. Machinery, skilled workers and experience all had to be collected. In all of Canada, there were only ten sets of gauges.

The Imperial Munitions Board
In the summer of 1915, David Lloyd George, a Welsh radical with great energy, became Britain's minister of munitions. Canada's Shell Committee turned out to be only a small part of Lloyd George's problems, but it was bad enough. Out of $170 million in orders, it had delivered only $5.5 million, most of it far behind schedule. The new British minister was blunt: without full reorganization, Canada would get no more orders. By the end of 1915, both London and Ottawa had worked out an answer. Hughes and his Shell Committee were pushed to one side. An Imperial Munitions Board, responsible directly to the British, would be set up in Canada. At its head would be Joseph Flavelle, a prominent self-made millionaire from the bacon-exporting business.

It seemed an odd choice, but it worked. Flavelle collected some of the brilliant managers who had been trained in the Laurier boom. He backed them up when they slashed the prices of some of the greediest contractors. He helped them enforce quality control on manufacturers who had even stooped to faking inspection stamps or filling pinholes with paint. When western manufacturers demanded more business, Flavelle had facts at his fingertips to show that they had not fulfilled the contracts they already had. He was just as ruthless with labour. When trade unions demanded higher wages, Flavelle told them their members were lucky to have jobs. When workers went on strike at munitions factories in Hamilton, Flavelle used the War Measures Act to ban reporting of the dispute.

By 1917, the Imperial Munitions Board had become the biggest business Canada had ever seen. It controlled 600 factories and employed a quarter of a million workers, including 40,000 women. Each day it did $2 million in business. By the end of the war, contractors and "national factories" built by the board itself had pro-

"We have been given new black boots, magnificent things, huge, heavy "ammunition" boots, and the wonderful thing is they don't let water in. They are very big, and they look like punts, but it's dry feet now."
Louis Keene on the British army boots which replaced the Canadian boots first issued to the CEF.

By the time the war ended a total of 14 million tonnes of shells and explosives had been fired.

duced cargo ships, airplanes, flying boats, chemicals and explosives as well as millions of artillery shells.

The growth of a huge munitions industry in Canada was no doubt the most spectacular development of the war years, but it was probably less important to the allied cause than some of the traditional staples Canada had always offered for export. Food was the most important. The war ended the shipments of Russian wheat that had begun to challenge Canada's exports to Europe. With millions of men in uniform and much French farmland behind the German lines, France and Britain needed all that Canadian farmers could produce.

It was a dangerous temptation for prairie farmers. The prewar droughts had warned them that their soil needed careful tending and that some regions were too dry for anything but ranching. Perfect growing conditions in 1915, the biggest crop in history and a limitless market in which to sell it sent caution out the window. Governments urged farmers to grow all they could and farmers, with prices climbing, happily did their best. After 1915, yields fell. Unthinking farmers were slowly creating the environmental disaster of the 1930s dustbowl. The war was their excuse.

Financing Canada's War

Within a year of the outbreak of war, Canada's contribution to the allied cause was established: men, munitions and food. All of them depended on money. The strain of financing the war would change the Canadian government almost beyond recognition.

Government in pre-war Canada had been a modest affair. Canadians paid no federal income or corporation tax. If the tariff was a big concern, it was because import duties met from half to two-thirds of the costs of government. As Robert Borden regularly complained, even the tiniest expenditure had to be debated and approved by cabinet ministers. Even senior civil servants could make no decisions.

With the war, everything changed. In the South African War of 1899-1902, Britain had paid for the small Canadian contingent. In 1914, Ottawa proudly insisted that Canada would bear the full cost. No one even asked how much money was involved. Peacetime accounting collapsed. Thomas White, the finance minister, later admitted that his department lost control. Federal spending rose from $184.9 million in 1913 to $337.9 million in 1915, the first full year of war. By 1917, it had climbed to $573.5 million, with $344 million of it for military purposes.

Finance ministers had always insisted that governments pay their way. If revenues — based on duties and excise taxes — fell, so must spending. In the war emergency, the government took a very different tack. Duties and excises should increase, White admitted, so that everyone, rich and poor alike, could make sacri-

Crops
The war ended a prairie trend to mixed farming. Between 1914 and 1918, the amount of land planted in wheat rose from 23 million hectares to 39.8 million hectares. The huge 1915 crop prompted thousands of people, from real estate agents to plumbers, to buy or rent land. By 1917, inexperience, costly labour and soil exhaustion caused crop yields to shrink to half the 1915 levels. Soaring prices compensated farmers. The 1915 crop brought $325 million; the smaller 1917 wheat harvest earned farmers $405.7 million.

Opposite page:
Top left: Women work on building lifeboats at Baddeck, Nova Scotia. Right: Inspecting completed shells at a Toronto munitions factory. Bottom: Building a Curtiss flying boat. Flying boats were needed for anti-submarine patrols.

fices. However, the real cost of the war would be met by borrowing. Future generations could pay. "We are justified in placing upon posterity the greater portion of the financial burden of this war," White explained, "waged as it is in the interests of human freedom and their benefit. . . ."

The next question was who would lend the money? The British had all they could do to finance their own war effort. Since no one had ever asked Canadians to invest in their own country, White was convinced that it could never be done. The only remaining alternative was New York. But the price for American money was high. The need for it was growing greater all the time.

By rescuing the floundering munitions industry, Joseph Flavelle had done the Canadian economy a great favour. With his help and that of the great 1915 harvest, Canada was now booming. The real worry by the end of 1915 was whether Britain could afford to buy from her former colony, with her own credit pledged deeper and deeper to the New York banks. Flavelle now used his powerful influence as Thomas White's former employer to force the timid finance minister to see reason. The time had come, he insisted, to borrow from Canadians. Nervously, White agreed to seek $50 million in the Canadian market. Almost at once, he got $100 million. Half of it was gratefully taken over by Flavelle to finance the Imperial Munitions Board. Again in 1916 and 1917, bond issues brought in far more than White expected. In 1917, a first Victory Loan, designed for small savers and backed by patriotic appeals, was launched. The government hoped for $150 million; it got almost $500 million.

By 1917, Britain could buy no more. With her lack of credit, Canadian shells had become a luxury she could no longer afford. Once again, Flavelle's ingenuity worked overtime. So did his luck. On April 20, 1917, the United States finally declared war on Germany. While White kept the munitions factories going with money from his bond issues, Flavelle went to Washington to look for business. The Americans welcomed him as a fellow-spirit. Nearly as unready for war as Canada had been three years before, the United States needed almost everything that the IMB factories could produce. American money replaced British and the Canadian factories stayed in business. Indeed, it was American orders which broadened the IMB's production to include ships and aircraft.

Before the war, businessmen like Flavelle had often complained that governments were not run on business principles. By 1916, it was sometimes hard to see whether businessmen or politicians were in charge. When the government exercised its huge powers through the War Measures Act, it was businessmen who controlled the levers. When a government created a Wool Com-

Victory Bonds
By 1919, individuals and corporate investors had purchased $2 billion worth of victory bonds.

Oh please do! Daddy

BUY ME A VICTORY BOND

One of the major new ideas of the war was that governments could borrow from their own citizens. Victory bonds drew on the savings of ordinary Canadians. Posters like this brought in hundreds of millions of dollars.

mission or a Board of Grain Commissioners or a War Purchasing Commission, businessmen were appointed.

Business or Politics in War?

The enormous prestige Canadian business leaders had gained during the Laurier boom continued into the war years. Newspapers and magazines ran long, respectful articles on Canadian tycoons,

A blunt and practical appeal for men to join Canada's tiny wartime navy.

recorded their humble origins, their hard climb to the top and their solemn opinions on national questions. It does not seem to have occurred to Sir Robert Borden that other people might have had useful advice and leadership to offer. In wartime Britain, business leaders were also influential, but so were trade unionists and even an occasional socialist from the new Labour Party. Canadian labour leaders had no role in wartime policy-making. Neither did Laurier's Liberals. As a result, they became critics.

So long as Canadians seemed united about the war, there was little room for criticism or questioning. For those to whom it became a great moral crusade, the only question was who was most fully committed to the struggle. Those who complained or "played politics" strayed dangerously close to treason.

The truth was, of course, that not all Canadians cared deeply about the war. They could be sceptical about the propaganda of both sides and about the greatness of the issues at stake. Another wartime slogan, "business as usual," urged them to keep calm, work hard and, for that matter, to seek a profit even on the beef contract with a local military camp. Many prairies settlers from central Europe put up with insults about "enemy aliens," kept their sons away from recruiting sergeants and profited handsomely from wartime prices while the farms of patriotic but absent neighbours turned to weeds.

It should have been apparent that the sharpest resistance to the war effort would come from Quebec. The crowds in the streets had been deceiving. Laurier's "Ready, aye, ready" was not spoken for French Canada. In Borden's cabinet there was no strong voice to appeal to Quebec or even to explain to the prime minister that Catholic Quebeckers had no more love for the anti-clerical French Republic than they had for England. The French tricolour flag, which English Canadians routinely used as a symbol for their French-speaking neighbours, represented a revolution Quebec had rejected. It would be as sensible to appeal to English-speaking audiences by waving the American stars and stripes. Thanks to Hughes, there was no French-Canadian battalion in the First Contingent to give Quebeckers a sense of participation. That had to wait for the 22nd Battalion in the Second Contingent.

For French Canadians — though not for them alone — the World War was in fact a distant European war. Thanks to White's policy of not raising taxes, it did not cost them much and Flavelle's munitions factories soon created thousands of new jobs. The war mattered only if it affected Canada. In September 1914, Bourassa had briefly hoped Ontario might, as a gesture of national unity, repeal its Regulation 17 so that Franco-Ontarians might again have their own schools. That did not happen, nor did Sir Robert Borden even use the war as a pretext to argue with his fellow-Conservatives in Ontario. On the contrary, the war seemed to entrench prejudices against any sort of difference. By 1916, Manitoba and other prairie provinces had also abolished old compromises that permitted French and other languages to be used in their schools.

English-speaking Canada was now preoccupied with the war. Gradually Bourassa and the ardent young nationalists who surrounded him defined a different struggle. While other Canadians condemned Prussian militarism and tyranny, Bourassa would focus on the plight of the French-speaking minority of Ontario.

The crusade took time to get rolling. Financial appeals in Quebec to send money to "the wounded of Ontario" brought little cash. Even the Franco-Ontarians were divided, wondering whether Bourassa's angry speeches might cause more harm than good. Laurier's Liberals, growing confident of victory in the next election, worried that Henri Bourassa had found a new way to split their party.

The fact remained that, by 1916, there were two war efforts at work in Canada: Bourassa's and Borden's.

Although Henri Bourassa served in Parliament from 1925 to 1935, his influence as a Quebec politician never regained its wartime height. He died in 1952.

REVIEW AND DISCUSSION

Key People and Ideas
Explain the importance of each of the following people and ideas as they are discussed in the chapter.

Sam Hughes	The War Measures Act
Joseph Flavelle	The Canadian Expeditionary Force
J. W. Dafoe	The Canadian Patriotic Fund
Arthur Meighen	The Imperial Munitions Board

Analysing the Issues
Answer each of the following questions, which deal with important issues raised in the chapter.

— What countries formed the two rival alliances in World War I?
— Why did most Canadians believe that the war would be "over by Christmas"? Why did it not, in fact, end this quickly?
— What factors caused the pacifist movement in Canada to dissolve when the war began?
— What factors led to the widespread opposition in the province of Quebec to Canada's involvement in the war?

Questions for Discussion
Think carefully about each of the following questions and discuss the issues they raise.

— Was Canada's treatment of "enemy aliens" proper, considering that the country was at war? If not, how should the problem have been handled?
— The finance minister, Sir Thomas White, asserted that "we are justified in placing upon posterity the greater portion of the financial burden of the war, waged as it is in the interests of human freedom and their benefit . . ." Was White's policy of paying for the war by borrowing against future revenues a good one? What other alternatives were available to him?

3

SUPREME SACRIFICE

Once the Canadian soldiers crossed the Atlantic, they became part of the British army. Although Canada's Militia Act allowed its members to serve outside Canada, men of the Canadian Expeditionary Force enlisted under Britain's Army Act. Now, they needed training and equipment. For four months the Canadian Contingent camped on Salisbury Plain in southern England in the wettest winter in memory. Tents blew down and men and horses were rarely dry. A British general, Sir Edwin Alderson, took command of the Canadians, weeded out the worst of Hughes's misfits and organized his men into a fighting division.

Much of the equipment which Canadian contractors had so profitably supplied was scrapped, to be replaced by more rugged British equivalents. One item was the MacAdam shovel, named for Hughes's secretary, Ena MacAdam, who held the patent. It was an odd contraption with a short handle and a big heavy blade to be used either for digging or as a shield. When a colonel found that the blade would not even deflect a bullet, the soldiers got rid of them. They would gladly have got rid of their Ross rifles as well, but the hard-pressed British did not have enough Lee-Enfields to replace them.

Later, friends of Sam Hughes claimed that he had stormed into the British war minister's office to protest plans to break up the Canadian contingent. This is nonsense. There were no such plans. The British knew that the Canadians would fight better if they stayed together.

Learning About War

As soldiers, Canadians had everything to learn. Military law promised death by firing squad for desertion, striking an officer, even cowardice. They found that they were now part of a huge organization. Their little platoon of forty men under a lieutenant was part of a company. Four companies formed a battalion, and soldiers soon learned that their battalion — the 3rd Torontos or the 15th Highlanders — would be their "family" for the rest of their service. Four battalions formed a brigade and three brigades a division, commanded by a major-general. Divisions also had their own batteries of artillery and companies of engineers. An army medical corps looked after the sick and wounded, and an army service corps delivered food and ammunition.

This and much more Canadians learned as they marched and drilled, dug trenches and fired their rifles under the driving winter rain of Salisbury Plain. The rest they could learn only in France. On February 4, the new 1st Canadian Division paraded for King George V, and on February 16 the first units landed at Saint-Nazaire in France. Others formed the Canadian Cavalry Brigade to wait for the day when men on horseback might again win battles. Thousands more waited in Canada until they were needed as replacements for killed and wounded. Some of them were already needed. One battalion of the contingent, Princess Patricia's Canadian Light Infantry, had been formed from British army veterans living in Canada. In December the PPCLI had gone to France to learn the miserable, murderous business of trench warfare.

Opposite page: One of the horrible features of the battlefield was the stench of unburied dead. Soldiers from both sides lay mingled, corpses bloated by internal gases, covered by flies and gnawed by rats.

Opposite page.
Top: Soldiers stop for a mug of tea while stew boils in the camp cookers and ration parties wait to take food to the front lines.
Bottom: Loaded under 30-35 kilograms of kit, rifle and ammunition, a marching column was expected to cover five kilometres an hour for eight or ten hours at a stretch. A French woman sells food to men in the passing column.

Only one man had foreseen what the First World War would be like. In the 1890s, a Polish banker named Ivan Bloch warned that future wars would end in two long lines of trenches. Hundreds of thousands would die before generals admitted that modern weapons made attacks impossible. Wars would end only after one or both sides were utterly exhausted. Bloch's nightmare vision persuaded the Russian tsar to summon peace conferences at The Hague. Nations signed treaties promising to treat prisoners humanely and never to use horrifying weapons like poison gas. Realists snorted their contempt.

By the time Canadians reached the Western Front it was much as Bloch had predicted. A "no-man's land" pockmarked by shell-holes, with rusted barbed wire and fragments of equipment and human bodies, separated two thick systems of trenches. Machine guns swept the landscape from behind thick mounds of sandbags. Men crouched in deep dugouts, safe from all but a direct hit by heavy artillery shells. Sharp-eyed snipers waited in hiding for an unwary enemy to show himself.

In a quiet sector of the long front, Canadians learned the routine of trench warfare. Soldiers did most of their work after dark. Patrols headed into no-man's land to watch and sometimes fight the enemy. Working parties repaired barbed wire entanglements or rebuilt trenches destroyed by artillery or the frequent rain. Others went to collect food, water and ammunition, dragging it back along miles of communication trenches. An hour before dawn and again at dusk, every man stood guard because those were the favourite times for attack. In the daytime some men were allowed to sleep. Exhausted soldiers found they could sleep in a puddle of water, standing up and even on the march.

Out of the trenches, the infantry was supposed to "rest," but usually there were loads to carry, trenches to dig or boots and brass buttons to polish for a general's inspection. Occasionally, soldiers had their turn for a bath and clean underwear, but the body-lice that afflicted almost every soldier in France soon returned. "Chatting" or squeezing them out of the seams of clothing was a constant pastime. So was thinking about food. This was the first great war in history in which almost no soldiers starved, but their coarse diet of corned beef, tea and bread or biscuit left them always hungry. In rear areas, soldiers could escape to little French taverns or *estaminets* for their favourite treat, fried egg and chips.

In the trenches, there was no escape. Soldiers lived in rain and snow and always in the thick Flanders mud. Food was brought up from the rear in sandbags. Even the thin smoke from a pocket cook-stove drew artillery fire. Huge rats gorged themselves on leftovers and on the unburied corpses in no-man's land. Everyone was tired, but sleeping on sentry duty was an unforgivable offence.

Soldiers "stand to" in a front-line trench. Part of the routine of battle was to stand guard for an hour at dawn and at dusk, the likeliest time for an attack. Steel helmets were given to the soldiers in 1916, after many losses from head wounds.

Life was also dangerous. On their first quiet tours of trench duty the Canadians lost almost a hundred killed and wounded. In the germ-laden mud, almost every wound became infected. Medical care had made enormous strides before 1914, but antibiotics were twenty years away and even blood transfusions were still experimental. At dawn, weary mud-caked soldiers stood to, thinking only of the cigarette and the gulp of fiery army rum that might help them through to another night.

Breaking the Stalemate

Far behind the trench lines, generals on both sides schemed and dreamed about breaking the stalemate. It would be hard. All armies had prepared for a fast-moving war, with cavalry, light artillery and tactics that stressed attacking. Now they had to wait for factories to produce heavy guns and enough shells to pulverize enemy trenches and dugouts. Ancient weapons were revived. Two hundred years before, mortars had lobbed bombs over fortress walls. Grenades were bombs a soldier could throw with his own arm. Both came back to trench war. Flame-throwers, inspired by ancient Greek Fire, hurled flaming gasoline at an enemy dugout or concrete machine-gun post. Even armour returned from the middle ages when soldiers received steel helmets to protect them from head wounds.

Other inventions were entirely new. Horses still carried or hauled the army's supplies, but now trucks, buses and staff cars bounced along the cobbled roads. Huge tractors dragged heavy guns, and already Colonel E. D. Swinton had an idea for using caterpiller tracks to roll across the battlefield. In 1914, eleven years after the first flight, airplanes were still fragile, unreliable toys; by 1915, both sides had recognized them as a vital new weapon of war. German, French and British experts strained their ingenuity to improve engines and airframes. Young pilots struggled to fly and to fight in an element war had never entered before. Only aircraft and balloons allowed generals to see across the enemy's lines. Dramatic improvements in wireless and in aerial photography were necessary if information was to get back.

In most of the new technology of war, the Germans were the leaders. Cartoon images of stupid, stiff-necked German generals are wrong. Prewar Germany had outpaced its rivals in science and education, and the results paid off in wartime. German strategists were also smarter. While French and British generals wasted lives trying to break through the trench lines, the Germans began moving their armies eastward against Russia. The tsar's armies, short of artillery, machine guns and even rifles, would be worn down. First, however, the Germans would give the western allies a little surprise.

In mid-April, the Canadian division took over trenches in front of Ypres. It was a great honour. Surrounded on three sides by German trenches, Ypres was a last remnant of Belgium in allied hands. It was there in an earlier battle that British regulars had died in their thousands to stop the German offensive. Quietly, the Germans installed 5730 cylinders of chlorine gas in their front line. On a pleasant spring evening, April 22, they released the gas. A green cloud rolled toward the French-Algerian division opposite. Gasping and dying, clutching their throats, the soldiers fled. The Hague treaty was broken. So was the trench line.

That night, Canadians of the 3rd Brigade counter-attacked to close the gap. By dawn, they were driven back, leaving hundreds of dead and prisoners, but the Germans stopped. On the 24th, the Germans turned on Brigadier-General Arthur Currie's 2nd Brigade with more gas, artillery and massed infantry. Currie's leading battalions were destroyed. To breathe, soldiers urinated on their handkerchiefs and held them over their noses. Ross rifles seized up from the heat of rapid firing or jammed when they fell in the mud. Somehow, the men kept fighting and the Canadian line held. British, Indian and French soldiers finally arrived to help and the

"By degrees — as we put mile after mile behind us — the straps across our shoulders begin to cut most damnably; we try adjusting our packs, but it makes no difference. The rifle feels as heavy as a ship's mast and has to be shifted from one shoulder to the other; we march with drooping heads and bowed backs, sore from the tips of our toes to the hair on our heads."

Thomas Dinesen, a Danish-Canadian winner of the Victoria Cross, describes route-marching. Soldiers carried about thirty kilograms of gear as well as a rifle weighing almost five kilograms.

struggle lasted for weeks after the Canadians withdrew to rest.

The Second Battle of Ypres cost the Canadians 6035 men. The PPCLI, involved in a later stage, lost 678 of its thousand men. Official telegrams brought home the tragedy of war to a few thousand Canadian homes. Many more Canadians imagined the battle through romantic war paintings and boastful newspaper accounts and dreamed of military glory.

Overseas, memories of victory soon faded. At Festubert on May 18, the Germans pulled back slightly and then devastated advancing Canadians caught in the barbed wire. The division lost 2468 men and gained nothing but experience. At Givenchy on June 15-16, explosion of a mine under the German trenches was to signal the attack. By mistake, the explosion blasted Canadians as well as Germans and the assault failed with heavy losses.

A Canadian Corps

In the spring, a second Canadian contingent had reached England after a winter spent scattered across Canada in drafty exhibition halls and militia armouries. In September, the 2nd Canadian Division crossed to France and General Alderson took command of a new Canadian Corps. Two Canadian brigadiers, Arthur Currie and Richard Turner, took command of the 1st and 2nd Divisions respectively.

An army corps was composed of two or more divisions and was commanded by a lieutenant-general. Each division had a major-general in command. Currie was a former teacher and real estate agent from Victoria. Turner, who had won the Victoria Cross in South Africa, was in business in Quebec City.

If Sam Hughes had been allowed, he would have taken over the Corps. He was shocked by the losses at Ypres and furious that Alderson had finally replaced the Ross rifle with the Lee-Enfield. Hughes had despised British generalship in the South African war. Now, he raged, the generals were as hopeless against the Germans as they had been against the Boers. To Max Aitken, the ex-Canadian millionnaire who represented him at British headquarters, Hughes grumbled: "It is the general opinion that scores of our officers can teach the British officers for many moons to come." When Alderson formed his new headquarters, the minister insisted that Canadians fill the staff jobs. His own son, Garnet Hughes, became a brigade commander.

The Canadians, however, still had much to learn. The long, cold winter of 1915-16 was part of their training. The Canadian Corps stood guard in front of Messines Ridge. From the high ground, the Germans could see what happened in the Canadian lines. Even their sewage flowed down into the Canadian trenches. At the end of March, British commanders planned a new attack. A winter of tunnelling had placed seven mines under the German trenches. On March 27, the mines exploded and a British division took the smoking craters and held them. On April 4, Turner's 2nd Division took over in its first big battle, ready to hold off the fierce German counter-attacks.

Two days later, the German attack came. Canadian defences

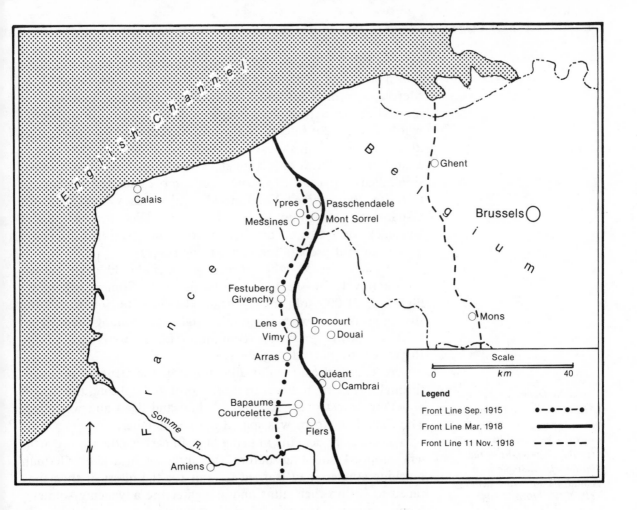

The Western Front

crumbled. Five of the craters were lost. Sheathed in mist and rain, Turner's men fought back in a bitter local struggle. Control of the muddy battlefield seesawed back and forth. Finally, on April 19, the Germans drove out the last Canadians. The division had lost 1373 men and the last of the craters. Why had the Canadians failed? Air photographs, taken in the rare intervals when the mist cleared, showed the shocking truth. Canadian staff officers had identified craters 6 and 7 as 4 and 5. Artillery had been ordered to fire on the wrong targets. Neither Turner nor his officers had gone forward to check.

Had they been British, they would have been dismissed. To fire Canadians, Aitken warned headquarters, would cause a political explosion. The British took the hint. General Alderson became the scapegoat. His successor, Lieutenant-General Sir Julian Byng, was a good choice. He took the raw Canadian Corps, moulded it into a big professional organization and gave it a unique approach to war. It took him a year.

Sir Julian Byng later served as Governor General of Canada from 1921 to 1926.

The Summer of 1916

In March 1916, a 3rd Canadian Division was formed from units like the PPCLI that were already in France or England. At Mont Sorrel on June 1, it had its baptism of battle. Major-General M. S. Mercer, a former Toronto lawyer, was in the front lines with his men when German artillery opened a deluge of fire. Bodies, even whole trees, were hurled in the air. Mercer was wounded, then killed. The few shell-shocked survivors could not stop the German assault troops. Next day, a quick counter-attack by Currie's division failed. Currie asked for more time, more guns and a chance to rehearse. Byng agreed. On June 13, after a heavy bombardment, Canadians swarmed up the little hill. It cost 8000 men to lose and win back Mont Sorrel, but both Currie and Byng had learned a lesson: careful preparation could bring success.

It was a lesson other British generals should have learned before July 1. On that day, the battle of the Somme began. By nightfall, 21,000 soldiers lay dead, the most terrible losses the British army ever experienced in a single day. Among them, lying thick as mown grass near Beaumont-Hamel, were men of the Royal Newfoundland Regiment.

A single, dreadful day did not stop the struggle to break through the German lines. In three months of fighting, the British and French lost over six hundred thousand dead and wounded. The Canadian Corps was spared until September.

Machine Guns

Machine guns had been used in war since 1870. It was the industrial revolution brought to the battlefield. A single man could mass-produce death. On July 1, 1916, at the Somme, German machine guns cost a single British division 218 out of 300 officers and 5274 of the 8500 other ranks. On the same day, the Newfoundlanders lost 710 men trying to cross 200 metres of mud.

There were benefits in being late. In earlier attacks, the artillery stopped shooting before the infantry attacked. German machine gunners had learned to wait for the interval; then they raced to set up their guns and slaughter the advancing soldiers. Now, artillery officers promised a rolling barrage, that would creep forward just in front of the attackers. It all depended, of course, on perfect timing and communications. There was also an exciting secret weapon concealed in huge crates marked "tanks." His Majesty's land ships, they were called, huge tracked monsters, armoured, with small naval guns, capable of a top speed of 5½ kilometres an hour, crossing three-metre-wide ditches, proof against any hail of machine gun bullets.

On September 15, 1916, as the British and Canadians got ready to attack Flers-Courcelette, both the artillery tactics and the tanks got their first trial. Frankly, the guns worked better. All six tanks with Turner's division broke down, but artillery fire pulverised the German front lines. French Canadians of the 22nd Battalion and Nova Scotians of the 25th fought their way into the village of Courcelette and held it against wave after wave of counter-attacks. "If hell is as bad as what I have seen at Courcelette," wrote Colonel Thomas Tremblay in his diary, "I would not wish my worst enemy to go there." Four days later, the 3rd Division finally took Fabeck Trench, but nothing the Canadians did could carry them to their final objective, Regina Trench.

On October 10, the 4th and last Canadian Division joined the

Corps. Its commander, Major-General David Watson, was a Quebec newspaper proprietor who had led a battalion at Ypres. Battlefield conditions were terrible. Shells had pulverised the chalky subsoil; autumn rains turned the dust to cement. Both sides were utterly weary. Everywhere that year, the war was going disastrously for the allies. A victory, however small, was needed. Watson's division must capture Regina Trench. It tried twice, with heavy losses, some of them the price of inexperience and poor communications. Finally, on November 11, 1916, a third attack went in. This time, artillery and infantry worked together. Regina Trench, "a mere depression in the chalk . . . for long stretches almost filled with debris and dead bodies," was taken.

It was enough for the year. The two months of fighting had cost the Canadians 24,029 casualties, the strength of a complete division. There was now a serious question whether Canada could find the men to fill the gaps.

Behind the Lines

By December, 1916, there were 108,000 Canadians in France and 135,000 in England. On the face of it, that was more than enough to meet the needs of the Corps. Unfortunately, Canadian administration in England was a mess. It had been so since Alderson took the 1st Division to France. By the fall of 1915, no fewer than three Canadian generals believed that Hughes had put them in charge. The eventual winner was Major-General John Wallace Carson, a Montreal stock promoter who had been sent to England with a vague mission to look after Canadian interests. Because he was a good friend of the minister, no one dared challenge him.

Hughes enjoyed the confusion. It meant that every big decision and most little ones had to be referred to him. Hughes's recruiting methods added to the problem. Sending hundreds of battalions to England when the Corps only needed forty-eight led to great bitterness when extra units were broken up. Hundreds of surplus officers, as angry as they were untrained, blamed staff officers not Hughes, for their embarrassment. Thousands of their men, untrained and unfit for service, clogged the Canadian camps.

Borden knew about the mess. His friend, Sir George Perley, acting Canadian High Commissioner in London, told him the bare facts. So did others. Twice the prime minister sent Hughes to England to sort out the mess. The minister thoroughly enjoyed the chance to inspect soldiers, instruct recruits in the rare art of bayonet fighting and lecture British generals on how to win the war. He even created a 5th Canadian Division in England for his son Garnet to command.

By September 1916, Borden had had enough. When Hughes finally returned to Ottawa, he discovered that his most cherished role was gone. Perley would become minister of the Overseas

Tanks
The idea of tanks was backed by Winston Churchill, who was First Lord of the Admiralty, when British generals showed no interest. Though they had a big impact on enemy morale, good tanks were (and are) hard to design. Engines, suspension, steering and armour all posed difficult technical problems. At Cambrai, when 324 tanks broke through the German line, 179 were out of action by night-fall thanks to breakdown, enemy shell fire or getting stuck in the mud. Tank crews risked burns and injuries from unguarded machinery or were poisoned by exhaust fumes.

Military Forces of Canada, based in London. For more than a month, Hughes raged, schemed and protested. Fed up at last, Borden dismissed his troublesome minister on November 9. One only wonders why he did not do it before.

In London, Perley faced a host of problems. Later, he admitted to Borden that he would never have taken the job if he had known just how bad the mess really was. Perley's recipe was simple: he brought to England the most respected officers he could find in the Canadian Corps and gave them full authority. Within months, the improvement was obvious. That did not mean that the Overseas Ministry lived happily every after. Fighting soldiers usually despise the staff officers who live safely in the rear, and Argyle House, the Canadian headquarters in London, was no exception.

Still, efficiency was a vital first step if Canadians were to control their own forces overseas. A few words in the order creating the Overseas Ministry changed the status of the Canadian Expeditionary Force. Suddenly, it was no longer part of the British army but an overseas contingent of Canadian militia. Perley had authority not just to clean up Hughes's mess in England but to get control over Canadians in France as well. Canadian soldiers would

Lieutenant Raymond Collishaw, one of Canada's greatest air aces, talks with a fellow pilot. Many Canadians joined the Royal Naval Air Service. Others served with the Royal Flying Corps. Both services were united in 1918 as the Royal Air Force. A quarter of RAF pilots were Canadian.

still serve under British command but as allies, not as colonials.

The change reflected the greater role Canadians as a whole were playing in the war. By early 1917, as Perley's ministry took shape, there were four infantry divisions and a cavalry brigade in France. Canadian doctors and nurses cared for British troops in the Mediterranean. Thousands of young Canadians now served in the newest element of the war, the air.

War in the Air

Sam Hughes, imaginative in much else, considered airplanes to be toys and refused to consider a Canadian air force. Hundreds of young Canadians disagreed. Even when they had to pay for their own training at schools in Toronto and Vancouver, they qualified as pilots and went to England to enlist. The new British flying services welcomed them. In 1917, the Royal Flying Corps began recruiting and training pilots and mechanics in Canada. On April 1, 1918, when the British united their army and naval flying services in a new Royal Air Force, 22,000 Canadians were in its ranks. They did every kind of flying duty, from spotting German submarines to flying heavy bombers over Germany. Those trained in Canada won a special reputation for skill and daring.

The stars of aviation were fighter pilots. Nowhere did technology move faster or with more deadly consequences. Every few months the best aircraft in the skies was outclassed by a better design or a stronger engine. The Germans, with superior technology, were usually in the lead. With often inferior planes and a wind that pushed them behind German lines, British and Canadian pilots suffered heavy losses. Only a few skilled pilots survived, downed five or more enemy aircraft and became "aces." Of the top twenty-seven British aces, ten were Canadians. The best of them, with seventy-two victories, was Lieutenant-Colonel Billy Bishop. Among all the aces of the war, he ranked third. The fifth, with sixty victories, was Major Raymond Collishaw. Three Canadian flyers, including Bishop, won the Victoria Cross for extraordinary gallantry.

Canada and the Submarine War

The Borden government's policies after 1911 denied the Canadian navy much role until the final year of the war. The two thousand Canadians who wanted to serve at sea had to join the Royal Navy. They found themselves part of as dangerous a struggle as any on the Western Front. Britain used her naval dominance to blockade Germany and her allies, barring all but a thin trickle of vital raw materials. A weapon as revolutionary as the airplane or the tank allowed the Germans to reply in kind.

In the first weeks of the war, admirals had been appalled when battleships were sunk by a single torpedo from a submarine.

"It was rather delicate work flying so close under the swift Hun, but he had no idea that I was in existence, much less sitting right below him. I carefully picked out the exact spot where I knew the pilot was sitting, took careful aim, and fired. Twenty tracer bullets went into that spot. The machine immediately lurched to one side and fell."
    William A. Bishop V.C.
    Canadian air ace

Canadian Flyers
One of the unexplored questions of the war is why Canadians did so well, contributing a very high share of the Royal Air Force's victories. Since most Canadian flyers came from the cities, there is little truth to the notion that young men from the Dominion profited from an open-air life, cold baths and plenty of practice shooting game. One reason was that Canadians spent more money on training than the British; another was that humble origins were no barrier to becoming an officer.

Primitive and unreliable as submarines were, no way yet existed to find a one unless it surfaced. Soon, Germany was sending its underwater fleet against even more valuable prey than battle-ships — merchant shipping. By mid-1915 when American protests forced the Germans to pull back, Britain had been squeezed by a German blockade. Early in 1917, Germany accepted the risk of the United States declaring war and resumed unrestricted submarine warfare. The gamble almost worked.

With no real warships, Canada could only help fight the sub-marine threat indirectly. In 1916, the first of 22,000 men of the Canadian Forestry Corps began cutting wood in Scotland and then in France. Millions of tons of timber would not have to get through the German blockade. Another vital cargo was feed for the horses that transported most of the army's needs. A Canadian, Jack Stewart, had an alternative: light railways could carry sup-plies right to the front lines, and who knew more about railway-building than Canadians? By the war's end, Brigadier-General Stewart's Canadian Railway Troops had built and run a vast net-work of railways behind the British line. It was often dangerous work. Stewart's 20,000 men lost 1977 dead and wounded.

Vimy Ridge and Hill 70

In 1916, the allies experienced disaster after disaster. The French army at Verdun and the British army at the Somme suffered huge losses. In the East, the Russian armies crumbled for lack of leader-ship and equipment; their allies could supply neither. Even the Turks, once despised by European powers, defeated British armies at Gallipoli, Kut-Al-Amara and in the Sinai desert. Roumania had briefly joined the allies only to be defeated in a matter of weeks. Germany seemed close to victory. Soon she would seem even closer.

Canada's main contribution to the war remained her Corps. Civilians would find the men and money to keep the divisions in the field; the soldiers would make the supreme sacrifice. They would fight better now with experience and the incessant training Byng imposed on his men. They could even laugh more. Soldiers of the 3rd Division formed a troupe to sing, put on skits and even perform as female impersonators. They called themselves the Dumbells, from the division's badge. The patriotic songs of earlier war years were embarrassing now: men roared out the choruses of "Oh What a Lovely War" or "When this Bloody War is Over".

There was a grimmer side. In 1916, the first few Canadians had been shot for desertion. There would be twenty-five such tragic cases before the war ended, but most men knew that, some-how, they would soldier on to the end — or until a "Blighty," a wound that would make them unfit for further fighting.

Although ships were registered in Canadian ports, Canada's merchant fleet flew the British red ensign and the British Admiralty assumed control at the outbreak of war. It was a reminder to Canada of her status as a colony.

"I had the familiar feeling of nervousness and physical shrinking and nausea at the beginning of this fight, but by the time we were halfway across No Man's Land, I had my nerve back. After I had been hit, I remember feeling relieved that I hadn't been hurt enough to keep me from going on with the men."

Alex McClintock on a night patrol

In the winter of 1916-17 — the coldest in twenty years — the Canadians faced Vimy Ridge, a long whale-shaped hill that rose from the Douai Plain. It remained securely German even after several British attacks. It would be the Canadians' first objective in 1917.

If victory took preparation, Byng would be ready. A huge model of the ridge was prepared and soldiers walked over it. Artillery massed in the rear and soldiers learned how to fire German guns so they could turn captured artillery on the enemy. Miles of tunnels, bunkers and dugouts were built and stuffed with stores and ammunition. Signallers buried twenty-one miles of cable seven feet deep. A chemistry professor from McGill University, Colonel Andy McNaughton, taught artillerymen how to pinpoint German guns by their flash and sound. Then, systematically, the enemy guns were destroyed. Byng backed his own attack by twice the artillery he had had in 1916 and trained the gunners to fire just in front of the advancing infantry.

Soldiers hurriedly set up machine guns during the capture of Vimy Ridge. The Vickers machine gun weighed 40 kilograms, fired 250 rounds a minute and was used by Canadians in both world wars and Korea.

"We went over the Ridge just at dusk and found it a jungle of old wire and powdered brick and muddy burrows and remnants of trenches. . . . Three dead men were reclining in the place, lolled back to the muddy wall, gazing incuriously before them, their faces turned black."
    Will R. Bird on Vimy Ridge

On Easter Monday, April 9, 1917, all four Canadian divisions rose from their trenches and walked right behind the exploding shells. They found the Germans still in their front-line dugouts. Beyond, the fighting was sharper and hundreds fell, but by 8 A.M. the 3rd Division was down the far side of the ridge. The 1st and 2nd Divisions took longer and the 4th Division, on the crest of the ridge, had the toughest fight of all. By April 12, the capture was complete.

Vimy Ridge was Canada's greatest achievement of the war and one of the greatest in her history. It was a triumph of courage over terrible danger, but it was a victory of other qualities too — discipline, foresight, ingenuity, hard work — virtues it had taken time for the Canadian Corps to develop. Vimy Ridge was a tragedy too. Men from every part of Canada had gone forward together and 3598 of them had died. Today, at the top of the ridge, soaring on the skyline, stands Canada's greatest memorial to her war dead.

After Vimy, Byng was promoted to command one of the five British armies. There was only one possible successor: Sir Arthur Currie. Borden, eager to pacify a still-troublesome Sam Hughes, asked Currie to accept Garnet Hughes to command the 1st Division. Currie refused: the ex-minister's son was incompetent. Borden subsided; Sam Hughes did not. For the rest of his life, Hughes spread and repeated charges against Currie which reverberated long after the war was over. Politicians did little to defend Currie's reputation and they could do nothing to silence Hughes. It was simply an added burden for a man with 125,000 Canadian lives on his hands.

How Currie would protect those lives was soon apparent. As a corps commander he had orders to obey, but sometimes those orders might be adjusted to win a bigger victory and to save lives. In August, the Canadians were given a new objective, the mining town of Lens. It would be a murderous battle but Currie had a suggestion. Lens was flanked by hills from which the Germans would pour fire on the advancing Canadians. If the Canadians took one of them, Hill 70, the Germans would try to take it back in the face of all the artillery the Corps could muster. Sir Douglas Haig, the British commander-in-chief, approved. On August 15, as 500 drums of blazing oil created a smoke screen to hide the advance, two Canadian divisions took the hill. Then, as Currie had expected, the Germans sent twenty-one successive counter-attacks against the hill. Each one was destroyed by Canadian artillery and carefully placed machine-guns. The battle cost Canadians 9198 dead and wounded. German losses were 20,000. By the grim standards of the war, it was a victory.

Horror at Passchendaele
The Canadian battles were diversions, first for a French offensive

that failed miserably, then for the British drive toward Passchendaele Ridge. This was perhaps the most dreadful battle of the war. Haig claimed that his objective was the German submarine bases on the Belgian coast, with their growing stranglehold on Britain. If so, his campaign was doomed from the start.

The British attack lay across reclaimed marshes. Four million shells destroyed the drainage and created a bottomless mire. Autumn rains, the heaviest in years, completed an almost impassable obstacle. Men, supplies, even artillery guns disappeared under the mud. The Germans, in concrete blockhouses on high ground, had the attackers at their mercy. Often the British could only advance in single file along wooden walkways. Wounded men drowned helplessly. In four weeks, General Hubert Gough's Fifth British Army lost 68,000 men. The morale of every unit in the Passchendaele campaign was shaken. In October, Passchendaele Ridge was still German.

Haig summoned the Canadians. Currie protested. He knew the ground. It was the same front Canadians had held at Ypres in

Working parties cross the sodden battlefield of Passchendaele. Many of the men carry "duckboards," portable wooden walkways. Wounded soldiers drowned in the deep mud and the flooded shellholes of the battlefield.

1915. The battlefield was horrible beyond imagination. To cross it and win the heights beyond would cost 16,000 men. Haig insisted. Currie made conditions. If he had to take over the mired artillery, every missing gun must be replaced and each one must be mounted on a firm wooden platform. There must be time to build roads up from Ypres. Haig glumly agreed.

For Canadian soldiers, shivering under groundsheets, nauseated by the sickly-sweet smell of decaying bodies, Currie's efforts probably meant little. On October 26, the first attack by the 3rd and 4th Divisions cost 2500 men. Four days later, the two divisions went only 100 more yards and lost 2731 men, but at least the ground was dryer. Currie took a week to switch the 1st and 2nd Divisions into the front line, repair roads and bring up more guns. At dawn on November 6, the final attack began. Guns and infantry worked together now, as they had at Hill 70 and Vimy. The ridge was taken. The price was almost what Currie had predicted, 15,654 casualties. On November 16, the Canadian Corps began to return to its old positions at Vimy and Lens.

Far to the south, Julian Byng had shown what the British army might have done. On November 20, a mass of four hundred tanks smashed into the German lines at Cambrai. A thousand guns crashed shells on the German defenders. Most gave up or fled. A six-mile gap was opened, but Byng had too few men to fill it. The Canadians he had asked for had been torn apart at Passchendaele. Only the Canadian Cavalry Brigade was available, as part of the British Cavalry Corps. At the end of the month, the Germans counter-attacked, filtering through the gaps in British defences. At Masnières, Canadian cavalry from Winnipeg and men of the Newfoundland battalion fought valiantly but in vain.

The defeat at Cambrai was all the worse because the hopes raised had been so high. Now both sides had lessons to learn. The British had shown that tanks could smash an enemy line but they needed infantry help. In their counter-attack, the Germans had avoided the strong points and moved deep into enemy territory, spreading panic among those who did not expect to fight.

Now there would be a race to see which side could use its new tactics first and best.

"Rats were everywhere, great podgy brutes with fiendish, ghoulishly gleaming eyes. They came at night on the parapets and startled one so that he thrust at them with his bayonet, or crawled over him as he lay under his blanket in his bunk, trying to 'shiver himself warm.'"
Will Bird

"It's all arranged for you, if there's a bit of shell or a bullet with your name on it, you'll get it, so you've nothing to worry about."
Louis Keene, a Canadian soldier, describes the philosophy of the trenches.

REVIEW AND DISCUSSION

Key People and Ideas

Explain the importance of each of the following people and ideas
as they are discussed in the chapter.

Ivan Bloch   No Man's Land
Arthur Currie   The Second Battle of Ypres
Sir Julian Byng   Battle of the Somme
George Perley   Hill 70
Billy Bishop

Analysing the Issues
Answer each of the following questions which deal with important issues raised in the chapter.

— What were the conditions faced by Canadian soldiers in the
  trenches of the Western Front?
— What factors led to the dismissal of Sam Hughes from his
  post as minister of militia?
— What factors led to the Canadian victory at Vimy Ridge?

Questions for Discussion
Think carefully about each of the following questions and
discuss the issues they raise.

— Why did the war along the Western Front lead to so many
  casualties? What alternatives were available to the commanders which might have reduced the number of
  casualties?

4

CONSCRIPTION

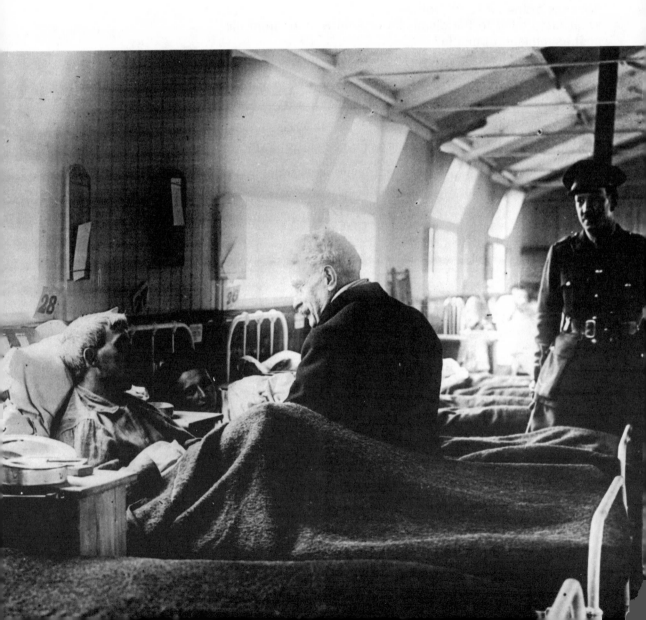

On the way back from Passchendaele, men of the Canadian Corps paused to vote. Few had heard of the party for which most of them voted. Some soldiers had only lived a few months in Canada. It did not matter. As they saw it, the issue in the election was as simple as a soldier's life: would Canada support them or would they be left to their fate? Ballots cast, the men formed their long columns and tramped down the road to Arras to see what their fate would be.

In Canada, the 1917 election was much more complex. Life for most Canadians had not been reduced to the stark simplicity of the front line. Still, the election of December 17, 1917, was a clearer choice than most: would Canada continue its utter commitment to victory? That question split the country as nothing had before. Commitment could no longer be measured by the words of politicians. The war effort was more than the profitable work of munition factories and farms. The war could only be won if more men could be found to risk their lives as soldiers.

Recruiting Volunteers

In 1914, recruiting had been easy. More men volunteered for the first two contingents than the government could use. Leaving New York for his first wartime visit to England, Sam Hughes had boasted to reporters: "We could send enough men to add the finishing touches to Germany without assistance from either England or France." In December, a more somber prime minister had warned a Halifax audience that two or three times as many men might be needed: "Canada will answer the call as readily and as fully as its men volunteered since August. There has not been, there will not be, compulsion or conscription."

In October 1914, Ottawa raised the ceiling on enlistments to 50,000. By July 1915, it had reached 150,000. In August, Borden paid his first wartime visit to London. He was appalled by the lack of energy and commitment among British leaders. Only the dynamic Lloyd George seemed wholehearted about the war. Canada could set an example. On his return, Borden raised the recruiting target to 250,000 men. Next, without consulting most of his cabinet colleagues, he used his New Year's message to announce that Canada would send half a million of her men to win the war.

How were the men to be found? At Valcartier, Hughes had summoned idealists and the unemployed. Sixty percent of the First Contingent were British-born, and almost half came from the badly depressed West. A special case was the famous PPCLI, organized with $100,000 contributed by Hamilton Gault, a Montreal millionaire.

After the First Contingent, General Gwatkin turned to Canada's pre-war militia regiments. They provided the best available recruiting system. The militia had units all over Canada. It had

Opposite page:
Sir Robert Borden visits Canadian wounded in 1917. The prime minister spent every possible moment bringing messages from home to men in hospital. Their sacrifices helped persuade him that conscription would be necessary.

whatever little military knowledge Canadians possessed. Some regiments had become wealthy private clubs and most had solid community support. In the cities, being a militia officer brought great social prestige and rich men paid for the privilege. Now that money and influence would build the Canadian Expeditionary Force.

Between October 1914 and September 1915, seventy-one new CEF battalions were authorized. The old militia regiments recruited the men and helped pick the officers. The system was not perfect. Since most of the best officers and almost all the modern equipment had left with the First Contingent, the new recruits got little training. Some waited months even for uniforms. Discipline was a problem. Some Ontario battalions dismissed more than 10 percent of their recruits as misfits. Many more deserted. Still, the system worked. In eleven months, the militia recruited 89,703 infantry volunteers. Only two battalions failed to fill their ranks. Best of all, the system cost Ottawa nothing. Raising a battalion cost about $13,000 but every penny came from local fund-raising or from private regimental funds.

There were critics. Enthusiasts formed Patriotic Associations or Civic Recruiting Leagues. Gwatkin's system did not satisfy them. By the summer of 1915 the patriots clamoured for government action, forcible registration of all able-bodied men, even conscription. The government neatly turned the tables on them. In September 1915, the Militia Department announced that any groups or individuals who wanted to raise CEF battalions could now apply to do so. Within three months, seventy-nine additional battalions had been approved. In 1916, seventy-nine more were authorized.

Recruiting became frenzied. By February 1916, three different battalions competed for men in Edmonton. In Winnipeg, there were six and in Toronto, ten. One unit promised mothers that none of its men would take a drink. Other battalions were reserved for "Sportsmen," Methodists or Orangemen. Many promised Scottish uniforms. Two were reserved for Americans who crossed the border and another was limited to "Bantams," men too short for the official height minimum. A Montreal regiment, more practical, promised warm clothing for the winter and boasted that it would be "the last to leave and the first to gain from victory." Some offers of service were rudely rebuffed. Battalions of Japanese or Black Canadians were not wanted. Canadian Indians, on the other hand, were eagerly sought.

Patriotic recruiting could be ugly in its prejudices. It also seemed to be successful, adding 123,966 men to the CEF's infantry battalions. The truth was more troubling. Of 170 battalions organized after October 1915, only 40 reached full strength. Almost 60 percent of the recruits (72,596 men) joined before the end of 1915.

Although Black Canadians had fought in the War of 1812 and served in the militia after the 1837 rebellions, they were not welcome in the CEF, and patriotic offers to raise a battalion were rejected because of racial prejudice. In 1916, a unit which became No. 2 Canada (Coloured) Construction Company was approved. Its members served in France with the Canadian Forestry Corps.

From July 1916 to October 1917, only 2810 men volunteered and went overseas as infantry. Even as Sir Robert Borden pledged his 500,000 Canadian soldiers, voluntary recruiting petered out.

There were many reasons. Thousands of Canadians bypassed the infantry to join the artillery, the engineers or the medical corps. Many joined forestry and railway units. After 1916, young Canadians could join the Royal Flying Corps in Canada. As it was, 232,968 Canadians volunteered for the infantry, one out of six Canadian men between fifteen and forty-four. As many more joined other branches of the CEF.

Those who did not had good reason. By the summer of 1915, two of the sharpest goads for enlistment had vanished. No one now believed that the war would be short and exciting. No one had to join the army to find work. Factory owners, desperate for labour, demanded that their skilled workers be sent home from overseas. In the West, which had sent far more than its share to the CEF, farm labour was now so scarce that wages soared. The worst enemy of recruiting was Canada's booming war economy.

Quebec and the War

Of course, that was not the only problem. If the West and Ontario had sent more than their share of young men to the war, Quebec

A recruiting office for a CEF battalion in Acton, a small Ontario town. The government left recruiting to local initiative, peacetime militia regiments and patriotic organizations. They found half a million volunteers before recruiting failed.

and the Maritimes had not. Again, there were hard, practical reasons. Obviously, single men found it easier to enlist: in Quebec and Atlantic Canada, men seemed to marry earlier. Rural areas, even in Ontario, found it harder to find recruits. Quebec and the Maritimes had many farm communities. Such facts were easily overlooked when another issue loomed so large: French Canada had not joined the national crusade.

Part of the fault lay with Ottawa. At Valcartier, it had never occurred to Sam Hughes that a French-speaking battalion might give Quebec a stake in the First Contingent. In the Second Contingent, General Gwatkin tried to repair the damage by including the French-Canadian 22nd Battalion. What he could not do was create the kind of militia organization in Quebec which built the CEF in Ontario or the West. When Ottawa tried to create more French Canadian battalions after the 22nd, few good officers volunteered.

Canadian Indians were eagerly sought as volunteers for the CEF, and by 1918 an estimated 35 percent of Indian men of military age were enlisted. However, because Indians were not considered full citizens, they were not subject to conscription in 1917, and true to its traditions, the council of the Six Nations insisted that any request for aid must come directly from the king.

Some historians have claimed that Sam Hughes bungled recruiting in Quebec by putting a Methodist minister in charge. A few moments' checking would tell them that this claim is nonsense. There was no recruiting organization in Quebec or anywhere else until 1916. In desperation, the Militia Department brought back Colonel Arthur Mignault from France and gave him a staff and money. The $30,000 given to Mignault was the only contribution Ottawa ever made to voluntary recruiting. It was almost wholly in vain.

Embarrassed by Quebec's recruiting record, Liberals in Ottawa naturally blamed government stupidity. There was a Methodist minister, the same C. A. Williams who appalled Woodsworth by his recruiting zeal. He had agreed to work with a Catholic priest to encourage enlistment. When no priest would serve, Williams quietly resigned. The Liberals also insisted that Sir Wilfrid Laurier's speeches at rallies for the 22nd Battalion showed what could have been done. Laurier made only two such speeches, both of them very eloquent. Despite his efforts, the 22nd Battalion had trouble finding enough men. Other French-Canadian battalions were emptied to fill its ranks.

The fact was that French Canadians had little interest in the war. It was, Armand Lavergne told his friend, Sam Hughes, "a somewhat interesting adventure in a foreign country." Both Lavergne and Henri Bourassa insisted that French-speaking Canadians had enemies much closer at home: "the English-Canadian anglicisers, the Ontario intriguers, or Irish priests." Quebec's front line was at the Ottawa River, not in Flanders: its enemies, Bourassa insisted, were the *Boches* of Ontario and their Regulation 17.

The Ontario government could have cancelled or even suspended Regulation 17 as a gesture of wartime unity. Liberals were as adamant as Conservatives in refusing. In Parliament, the issue split both parties. Senator J. P. Landry, Conservative Speaker of the Senate, was forced to resign when he took up the Franco-Ontarian cause. When Ernest Lapointe, a Liberal, moved a resolution asking Parliament to press Ontario to end Regulation 17, English-speaking Liberals helped defeat the move.

The raging schools debate gave French Canadians an argument for staying out of the war. They hardly needed it. A few, like the fiery, unpredictable nationalist, Olivar Asselin, enlisted because they cared passionately about France. His battalion, the 163rd, and another raised among tough Gaspé fishermen, were among the few excellent French-Canadian units. Unfortunately, their men were needed to fill the ranks of the 22nd Battalion. Most Quebeckers simply concluded that the war was none of their concern. If Bourassa and Lavergne told them not to enlist, that was fine, but they had already made up their minds. By June of 1917, 450,000 men and women had joined the CEF; about 13,000 of them were French-speaking.

More Men Needed

By midsummer, 1916, it was obvious that recruiting had slowed to a trickle. Long before, General Gwatkin had warned that two divisions might be all that Canada could keep in the field. Now there were four, and each would need 20,000 able-bodied new soldiers a year to replace the dead and permanently disabled. Sam Hughes had ignored the problem. If the Australians had five divisions, Canada would have six. Only his dismissal prevented the 5th Canadian Division from going to France. At Sir George Perley's insistence, it stayed in England.

In Canada, the recruiting enthusiasts now revived their demand for conscription. Some tried another tack. Perhaps it was time to show a little good-will and friendship to Quebec as the price of getting her young men for the war. A *Bonne Entente* movement started, with visits, speeches and banquets at Quebec and Toronto. Nothing changed. The good will went sour. Colonel Lorne Mulloy, blinded in the South African War and head of the Hamilton Recruiting League, demanded conscription; so did Chief Justice Thomas Mathers of Manitoba. The arguments would soon be familiar. Volunteering took the best and bravest. It undermined industry when skilled workers joined up. Even Bourassa sneered at the English-Canadians for letting themselves be killed while immigrants took over their jobs and farms.

Caught between his no-conscription promise and the need for men, the prime minister found a compromise. A National Service Board headed by R. B. Bennett, the Calgary millionaire and Conservative M.P., would invite all Canadian men to register. At once, labour union leaders and Bourassa insisted that this was the first step towards conscription. Borden himself journeyed to

Nurses
2400 Canadian women went overseas as nurses. They served in England, France, Belgium, Greece, Egypt and Russia.

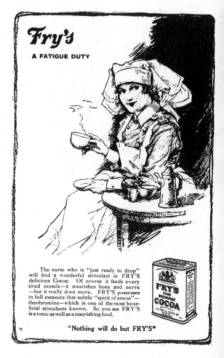

Fry's
A FATIGUE DUTY

The nurse who is "just ready to drop" will find a wonderful stimulant in FRY'S delicious Cocoa. Of course it feeds every tired muscle—it nourishes bone and nerve —but it really does more. FRY'S possesses in full measure that subtle "spirit of cocoa"— theobromine—which is one of the most beneficial stimulants known. So you see FRY'S is a tonic as well as a nourishing food.

FRY'S
PURE
BREAKFAST
COCOA

"Nothing will do but FRY'S"

While most Canadian feminists used the war years to serve in ways that governments and men regarded as appropriate, some women risked ridicule by learning to shoot, doing drill and seeking full equality as members of the fighting services.

Montreal to assure Archbishop Paul Bruchési that it was not so. More ominously, he refused to promise a delegation from the Trades and Labour Congress that he would never impose conscription. Nonetheless, the labour leaders as well as Bruchési's clergy dutifully joined patriotic groups in supporting a national registration. For their part, both Borden and Bennett insisted that it would be voluntary. At least a fifth of those who received cards took them at their word by never sending them back. Of the million and a half cards that did return, only 286,978 indicated men who might be suitable for service. Efforts to enlist them failed utterly.

Next the British took a hand. Borden's imperialism had always had two goals: aid and consultation. His pre-war naval policy had failed on both counts, but who could question the contribution Canada had made to the Empire since 1914. In 1915, Borden had had a glimpse of British wartime leadership and it appalled him. In London, his opinions were not sought and he got his war news from the newspapers. British ministers ignored Ottawa when they took over Canadian shipping or commissioned Montreal shipyards to build submarines.

When Borden demanded a voice for Canada, the response from the Canadian-born colonial secretary, Andrew Bonar Law, was blandly infuriating: "I fully recognize the right of the Canadian government to have some share in the control of a war in which Canada is playing so big a part," he confessed, "I am, however, not able to see any way in which this could practically be done . . . if no scheme is practicable, then it is very undesirable that the question should be raised." Law's polite dismissal enraged the Canadian prime minister. "It can hardly be expected that we shall put 400,000 or 500,000 men in the field and willingly accept the position of having no more voice and receiving no more consideration than if we were toy automata," Borden wrote to Perley. Then, shocked at his own anger, he tore up the letter.

A year later, there was a change. At the end of 1916, Britain's government was toppled. The new prime minister was the former Welsh radical, David Lloyd George. Old attitudes faded. Soon, Lloyd George summoned the dominion premiers to London. His reasons were blunt. "We want more men from them," he told his officials. "We can hardly expect them to make another great recruiting effort unless it is accompanied by an invitation to come over and discuss the situation with us." On March 2, 1917, most of the dominion prime ministers joined the new "Imperial War Cabinet" while other ministers met nearby in a larger Imperial War Conference.

Even Lloyd George would not share real power with colonial politicians, but he did give them alarming secret information. Russia was collapsing. The French army had mutinied. German submarines were strangling England. Only the British armies remained intact and they needed help. Lloyd George also promised a very different kind of Empire. Resolution IX, drafted by Borden and by South Africa's Jan Smuts, promised a postwar commonwealth of autonomous nations, with "an adequate voice' in Empire foreign policy.

Between meetings, Borden visited the Corps and every military hospital he could reach. For the first time he saw the long rows of wounded men. He learned that they would be sent back to the trenches until they were dead or so badly wounded that even army doctors would not pass them for service. In Canada, Laurier insisted that such men had chosen their fate; Borden could never agree. While he refused Lloyd George's request to send the 5th Division to France, Borden was now convinced that conscription was not only necessary but a moral duty. While he was overseas, the Corps took Vimy Ridge. The cost was over twelve thousand dead and wounded. That month, fewer than five thousand men joined the army.

On his dangerous voyage home past the German submarines, Borden's slow methodical mind digested the arguments. The Corps would need 75,000 more soldiers each year. In the camps in England and Canada there were fewer than 30,000. The national registration experiment had proved that qualified men would serve

Tom Longboat
Among the many Indians who served with distinction in the war was Tom Longboat (1887-1949), recognized for a number of years as the champion long-distance runner in America.

Armand Lavergne, 1880-1935, was Bourassa's ablest lieutenant. A lawyer, journalist and militia colonel, he was a personal friend of Sam Hughes. His political career took him successively from the Liberals to the Nationalists to the Conservatives. He was a Conservative M.P. when he died.

only if conscripted. Bourassa and Lavergne had claimed that Canadians would volunteer to defend their own country, but attempts to raise a 15,000-man home defence force attracted only 1000. On April 7, when the United States entered the war, her Congress immediately imposed conscription. If Canada was to play the new, independent role promised by Resolution IX, she could do no less.

The Military Service Act

On May 18, 1917, when Borden rose in the House of Commons, his case for conscription was ready. "All citizens are liable for the defence of their country," he insisted, "and I conceive that the battle for Canadian liberty and autonomy is being fought today on the plains of France and Belgium." At the end of the long speech, Borden's thoughts turned to the men he had left behind. "I know from my personal experience that they cannot realize the thought that their country, which summoned them to her service, will be content to desert and humiliate them."

Liberal politicians claimed that Borden introduced conscription as a popular issue to win votes. They even argued that he wanted to distract Canadians from the plight of the bankrupt Canadian Northern and Grand Trunk railways and his government's plans to nationalize them. This was nonsense.

Certainly Borden's party was in trouble. By 1917, every province but Ontario had defeated the Conservatives. Supporters and opponents of the war effort agreed that Borden's administration had been misguided, short-sighted and probably corrupt. But conscription was no guarantee of victory at the polls, and Borden knew it. Whatever letter-writers and newspaper editors might claim, conscription was not popular. In Australia, a far more united country than Canada, voters twice rejected it in plebiscites. Borden did not need his remaining French-Canadian ministers to tell him that Quebec would be bitterly opposed. So would the Trades and Labour Congress with its thousands of members in factories and in the coal mines of Cape Breton Island and the West. In Ontario and the prairie provinces, farmers would insist on keeping their sons and labourers on the land.

By mid-1916, French Canada's indifference to the war was hardening to anger. Recruiting parties in Montreal were attacked by crowds. In the spring of 1917, Pierre Blondin, Borden's postmaster-general, set out in a last bid to recruit volunteers in rural Quebec. He returned with only ninety-three men. Quebec's Catholic church was split. Archbishop Bruchési in Montreal sympathized with the government, but Cardinal Bégin in Quebec was coldly neutral; across the province, parish priests were now openly hostile. On May 24, a week after Borden's announcement, riots broke out in Montreal.

As in other arguments between French and English in Canada, no one listened to the other side. Borden insisted that Bourassa was a narrow-minded troublemaker, raising grievances that were petty by the scale of the world conflict. Bourassa saw the prime minister as an imperialist, sacrificing Canadian lives and money at England's command. Both men were nationalists but their views of Canada would never meet.

To Borden and to many English-speaking Canadians, Canada was fighting for herself, not for Britain. Bourassa believed that Canada's security, institutions and prosperity were safe behind the Atlantic moat. By all means use the war to get rich, Bourassa agreed, but that meant keeping men home to grow food and make shells. To Borden, such arguments were selfish and unworthy of Canada. The country must measure up to the heroism and self-sacrifice of her soldiers.

On how Canada met its responsibilities, Borden was prepared to be very flexible. Having announced conscription, the prime minister now approached Laurier to form a national coalition. The Liberal leader refused. Not unreasonably, he felt that the coalition offer might have come before Borden committed it to introduce conscription. Next, the prime minister offered to delay im-

Sir Robert Borden sits with other members of the Imperial War Conference of 1917. If Borden had a war aim for Canada, it was to win a guaranteed voice in imperial policy and world affairs.

posing conscription until a coalition government had won a general election. Again Laurier refused. He believed that his party would stick by him, and above all, he knew that if he allied himself with the Conservatives and conscription, he would again hand his own province to Henri Bourassa.

On June 11, the Military Service Act was presented to parliament. For two long months, it was debated. To hold his party together, Laurier pleaded that the question be put to all Canadians as a referendum. The government and many of his own English-speaking supporters dismissed the idea as merely a delay. Again and again the Liberal leader pleaded with the English-speaking majority, now united on conscription, not to drive a wedge through the unity of Canada. He opposed conscription, he insisted, "because it has in it the seeds of discord and disunion, because it is an obstacle and a bar to that union of heart and soul without which it is impossible to hope that this Confederation will attain the aims and ends that were in view when Confederation was effected." It made little difference. When the Military Service Act finally passed, twenty-five Liberals supported the government and nine French-Canadian Conservatives voted with Laurier. On August 29, conscription became law.

Despite the immense personal loyalty he inspired from his followers, Laurier had failed to hold his party together. An election was now inevitable, but Laurier still believed that the hope of victory would re-unite his party. As in the past, he misread public opinion in English-speaking Canada and, once again, he underestimated Robert Borden.

The Union Government

For the Conservative leader, the idea of a coalition was much older than conscription and his negotiations with Laurier. It had deep roots in his old discomfort with the party system, with the incessant squabbles over patronage and influence. Throughout the summer of 1917, aided by the deaf but influential Sir Clifford Sifton, Borden had reached out to second-rank Liberals. Some were interested, but still they were nervous and undecided. Borden turned back to Parliament and, using his Conservative majority, he armed himself with two powerful political weapons.

In 1915, the Liberals had opposed a Soldiers' Voting Act. Now it was redrafted as a Military Voters Act. Every man and woman in the CEF could vote. To solve the problem of running an election across the submarine-infested ocean, soldiers would vote simply for the government or the opposition. Those without close links to a constituency in Canada could choose one for themselves. Obviously, as the minister of justice sweetly explained, both parties would want to persuade soldiers to put their votes where they would do the most good.

Far more important and questionable was a Wartime Elections Act, devised by the increasingly influential Arthur Meighen. It gave votes to the wives, mothers and sisters of all who served or had served in the CEF. Such women, Meighen explained, would be able to vote for soldiers who had given their lives. It also took the right to vote away from Canadian citizens born in enemy countries and naturalized since 1902. Those who lost their votes would, however, be immune from conscription. Meighen did not need to add that such voters would, overwhelmingly, have supported the Liberals and had done so in three prairie provincial elections. Laurier and his furious and (for once) united party fought the act until Meighen's earlier device of closure was used to end the debate.

Both laws had their effect. Liberal confidence in victory began to dissolve. Prominent party members began to think again about those quiet invitations from Borden and his friends. On October 6, Parliament was dissolved. Canadians would vote on December 17. On October 12, Sir Robert Borden announced the formation of a Union government backed by every provincial premier except Sir Lomer Gouin of Quebec. A clutch of influential English-speaking Liberals, led by the Ontario party leader, Newton Rowell, nervously took office in the new government. An admiring Conservative admitted that he would match Borden against Job in a patience contest any day.

Borden understood that his patience would now be needed more than ever. Outside Quebec, newspaper editors solidly favoured the new government. Who could condemn a programme that promised full commitment to the war, reorganization of the railway system and a crusade against political patronage? There were other, more controversial reforms, but in the wartime Canada of 1917, their time seemed to have come. If elected, the Union government would be pledged to give votes to all women, not merely those favoured by Meighen's act. The old cause of prohibition would also triumph with a ban on the production and sale of beer and liquor. Wartime Canada could no longer afford the waste of labour and grain. In the patriotic mood, even Stephen Leacock (who despised women's suffrage as fiercely as he cherished his whiskey) would be silent.

Neither reform would be any more welcome in French Canada, than conscription. Borden's Union government lacked a single significant figure from Quebec. Not even a senator could be found. The lonely French-Canadian minister, Albert Sévigny, knew he would lose his seat though he did not yet realize that he would spend much of the rest of his life under police protection as an alleged traitor to his people. Quebec was now isolated and almost no one in English-speaking Canada seemed to care. Years of politely-masked resentment burst forth. "It is certainly not the

Clifford Sifton was one of those converted from opposition to women's suffrage by his own wartime speeches in defence of liberty and democracy. His cousin, Ida Sifton, pointed out the inconsistency of crusading for male liberty alone.

intention of English Canada'' warned *Saturday Night* magazine, ''to stand idly by and see itself bled of men in order that the Quebec shirker may sidestep his responsibilities.'' No one asked, of course, what role Quebeckers had played in assuming those responsibilities.

The 1917 Election

In October, the new Union government was confident of easy victory. As the weeks passed, that confidence faltered. In Ontario, the struggle to merge Liberal and Conservative ambitions in a single candidate led to battles in many ridings. In Nova Scotia and parts of the West, promises of Liberal support proved almost worthless. Rowell, the high-minded Methodist whom Borden chose as his Liberal lieutenant, was mistrusted by both parties. In British Columbia, Conservatives and Liberals utterly refused to co-operate with each other.

Borden's fears that conscription might be highly unpopular turned out to be right when Unionist politicians actually met the voters. At Kitchener, anti-conscription demonstrators howled

Behind the lines in Flanders, a Canadian soldier studies a Unionist poster appealing for votes. An overwhelming majority of soldiers voted for the government — 215,849 to 18,522.

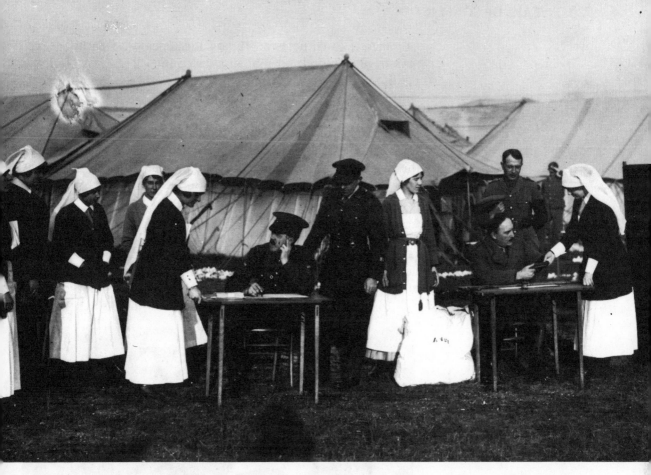

Borden off the platform for the first time in his political career. The new minister of militia, an ex-Liberal, found that farmers would vote for Laurier just to keep their sons at home. He promptly announced that all farmers' sons would automatically be exempted from the Military Service Act. The order was swiftly confirmed and Unionists in farming constituencies felt a wave of support. Another politically-inspired ruling directed that the brothers of serving soldiers would also be exempted. Aging parents would not be left without a breadwinner.

Such hurried gestures might have raised the question of whether the election was even about conscription. In mid-October, when the first class of conscripts was ordered to report, 93.7 percent applied for exemption and every man was sent home because Borden had promised that no one would serve until the election was over.

By election day, the Unionist campaign had degenerated into a crusade by patriotic English Canadians against a Bourassa-controlled Quebec. A vote for Laurier was a vote for the Kaiser. With all the promised exemptions, it was easy to argue that the Military Service Act would conscript only "slackers" and French Canadians. Sir George Foster, still Borden's Minister of Trade and

These nurses voting in 1917 were the first women to cast a ballot in a Canadian federal election. The wartime contribution of women helped overcome resistance to their political equality. So did confidence that most of them would back conscription.

Commerce, could declare: "Every alien enemy sympathiser, every man of alien blood, born in an alien country and every Hun sympathiser from Berlin to the trenches . . . wishes success to Laurier with his anti-conscriptionist campaign."

The outcome was the most one-sided election result Canada had yet seen: 153 seats for the Unionists, 82 for the Liberals and all but twenty of them in Quebec. Labour candidates, presented for the first time by an angry Trades and Labour Congress as an alternative to both Liberals and the Borden government, suffered humiliating defeats. Yet the result among voters was by no means as one-sided as the new House of Commons might suggest. With only the civilian votes, the Unionists led by a mere hundred thousand. Even outside Quebec, Laurier's Liberal candidates, with little money and almost no newspaper backing, collected 40 percent of the votes.

In March, the military vote was finally published. It added

Published in 1917, *Canada in Khaki* was subtitled: "A Tribute to the Officers and Men now serving in the Overseas Military Forces of Canada."

two hundred thousand to Borden's margin and changed the result in fourteen constituencies. Thanks to W. F. O'Connor, Chief Returning Officer for the election, most of the soldiers who had used the apparent loophole in the act to switch to a more crucial riding had their ballot set aside. The Liberals, outraged at the attempted fraud, overlooked the fact that it had been caught and stopped.

Born from a mixture of opportunism and idealism, the Union government now had all the authority it needed to run a divided Canada. For a generation, prominent English Canadian had called for an end to party politics. Others had denounced the concessions and compromises needed to conciliate French Canada. Others had promised a morally purified Canada once women had won the vote and liquor had been banned.

After December 17, their wishes could now come true.

Two women, Louise McKinney and Roberta Macadams, won seats in the 1917 Alberta election, becoming the first women members of a Canadian legislature. Louise McKinney was active in the Women's Christian Temperance Union in Alberta and owed her political prominence to her support for prohibition. One of her accomplishments, the Alberta Dower Act, guaranteed widows a share of their husband's estate.

REVIEW AND DISCUSSION

Key People and Ideas
Explain the importance of each of the following people and ideas as they are discussed in the chapter.

Olivar Asselin
Sir Andrew Bonar Law
Pierre Blondin
Archbishop Bruchési
Cardinal Bégin
Sir Clifford Sifton

22nd Battalion
National Service Board
Imperial War Cabinet
Military Service Act
Wartime Elections Act

Analysing the Issues
Answer each of the following questions, which deal with important issues raised in the chapter.

— What factors led to the decline in voluntary enlistments by 1916?
— What factors led to the low number of French Canadian volunteers?
— What factors led Sir Robert Borden to decide that conscription was necessary?
— What arguments did Laurier use to oppose the Military Service Act?

Questions for Discussion
Think carefully about the following question and discuss the issues it raises.

— Sir Robert Borden said: "All citizens are liable for the defence of their country, and I conceive that the battle for Canadian liberty and autonomy is being fought today on the plains of France and Belgium." Did Borden's arguments justify the introduction of conscription for overseas service?

5

WEARY OF WAR

By now, there was no use pretending that the war was going well. In March, 1917, the tsarist tyranny had crumbled. For a time it seemed possible that Russia would accept a parliamentary democracy. It might even have happened if the catastrophic war with Germany could have been ended. Instead, the last of the provisional governments was swept away early in November and Russia collapsed in a chaos of killing and civil war.

With Russia no longer a military threat, the German armies in the East could move westward against the French and British. Another ally was crumbling too. Italy had entered the war in 1915 in return for a promise of colonies and the satisfaction of fighting her old enemy, Austria. At Caporetto in 1917, Germans and Austrians had hurled the Italian armies back to the gates of Venice. Only powerful British and French reinforcements now kept the Italians in the war. As for the Western Front, Passchendaele and Cambrai had exhausted the British army and discredited its generals.

Even when there was success, military secrecy kept it hidden from the general public. After months of opposition, British admirals had finally agreed to organize Atlantic merchant shipping in big convoys instead of leaving each ship to run the gauntlet of German submarines alone. The results were amazing. With far fewer targets and most of them escorted by warships, submarine sinkings declined dramatically. American soldiers and supplies could now cross the ocean in relative safety. Unfortunately, the convoy system was a war secret civilians could not share.

Impact of War

By 1918, ordinary Canadians began to feel the hardships of war. After the 1915 harvest, the yield of prairie grain fell sharply. In 1917, Ontario urged its farmers to grow more food, but even thousands of school children and women volunteering as "farmerettes" could not harvest more than part of the crop. Food prices rose. War industries took more coal than the American mines could produce or than Canada's failing railway system could deliver. As a result, Canadians shivered through the winter of 1917 and now, in 1918, there would be fuelless Fridays and meagre stocks of coal for family furnaces.

The war brought home-front disasters. Halifax, fortified and garrisoned against surprise attack, and the port from which wartime convoys and most of Canada's soldiers departed, felt closer than most Canadian cities to the war. Nothing prepared it for the morning of December 6, 1917. A Belgian relief ship moving down the harbour clanged foolishly into the *Mont Blanc*, crammed with munitions of war. Sparks started a fire. As British and Canadian naval parties desperately fought the flames, the greatest man-made explosion to that time devastated Halifax's old wooden houses. As

Opposite page: Canadian soldiers enter the smouldering city of Cambrai during the offensives of the "Last Hundred Days." Despite some of the heaviest losses of the war, the Canadian Corps led the allied advance.

Opposite page: The
explosion that
devastated Halifax on
December 6, 1917,
damaged every building
in the city and broke
windows at Truro, 97
kilometres away. An
anchor shaft from the
Mont Blanc weighing
half a tcnne was hurled
three kilometres across
the North West Arm.
Except for it and a
cannon, the ship was
reduced to fragments of
steel that fell like hail
on the city's north end.

Cars on the Prairies
*Prairie farmers were big
buyers of cars. While
tractors were too big and
expensive to replace teams
of horses, a Model T or a
Maxwell could slash the
time it took to drive into
town. In the war years, car
registrations in Alberta and
Saskatchewan rose five-
fold. Tractor farming
would wait for
development of a small,
efficient gasoline-powered
machine.*

people beyond the immediate destruction rushed to their windows, the back-blast drove in the glass, blinding hundreds. Next day, a driving winter storm blanketed the city in snow, cutting off train-loads of medical aid. The Halifax explosion took 1,630 lives and left thousands maimed.

Somehow, the stricken city struggled back to life. It had to. In 1918, Halifax really was the front line in a new campaign. Frustrated by convoys, newer long-range German submarines crossed the Atlantic to attack North American shipping. The Royal Canadian Navy now had an urgent purpose, but the ships of its Halifax patrol were ill-equipped trawlers, commandeered for service. It was the Americans who sent real warships and a squadron of flying boats under the future Antarctic explorer, Richard Byrd.

The war years had not been bad for all Canadians. After mid-1915, men and women could find all the work they wanted. Poverty in Canada had always been due more to unemployment than to low wages. Many people found that for the first time in their lives they had a little money to spend on furniture, new clothing and even those Victory Bonds with their three percent interest. Wealthy people did much better in an age when there were no taxes on income. In 1916, a modest car cost $1500 or $2000, far more than a worker could earn in a year. During the war years, car ownership more than tripled from the 70,000 on the roads in 1914.

The good times could not last. The competition between consumers and war needs had to force prices up. So did Sir Thomas White's policy of making unborn generations pay for the war. In 1917, after modest increases in 1915 and 1916, the cost of living suddenly soared by 18 percent. Canadians were appalled. They had no experience of living with inflation. The belief that millionaires could manage the nation's affairs as well as their own was badly shaken. Newspaper editors demanded the conscription of wealth and the punishment of profiteering.

Of all the millionaire-managers of the war effort none was better known than Sir Joseph Flavelle, now a baronet because of his work with the Imperial Munitions Board. In December 1916, Flavelle had returned from France deeply moved by the sacrifices he had seen, shaken by the devastating effects of defective shells on the young men who served the guns. His report to a meeting of munition contractors was received in glum silence. Finally, one of them complained that they had come to hear about profits, not production. Flavelle exploded. "Profits? Send profits to the hell where they belong." Most Canadians cheered. Soon, they jeered. W. F. O'Connor, asked by Borden to find out why living costs were rising, reported that Flavelle's own bacon-exporting business had made huge profits. Some of O'Connor's facts were wrong and Flavelle had had little to do with the firm since 1914, but his reputation was destroyed. The president of the Trades and Labour

va Scotia's
n-the-War
wspaper

THE HALIFAX HERALD

ALL THE NEWS.   HONEST VIEWS.   HONEST ADVERTISING.

Nova Scotia's
Win-the-War
Newspaper

ED FEBRUARY 14, 1875.   HALIFAX, CANADA, FRIDAY, DECEMBER 7, 1917.   VOLUME XLIII. NO. 290.

HALIFAX WRECKED

More Than One Thousand Killed In This City, Many Thousands Are Injured And Homeless.

MORE than one thousand dead and probably five thousand injured, many of them fatally, is the result of the explosion yesterday on French steamp Mont Blanc, loaded with nitrocerine and trinitrotuol. All of Halinorth and west of the depot is a mass ruins and many thousands of people homeless. The Belgian Relief steamer Imo, coming n from Bedford Basin, collided with the Mont nc. which immediately took fire and was headed in Pier No. 8 and exploded. Buildings over a great a collapsed, burying men, women and children. Tug ts and smaller vessels were engulfed and then a t wave washed up over Campbell Road. Fires ke out and became uncontrollable, stopping the k of rescue. Not a house in Halifax escaped some age, and the region bounded on the east by the or, south by North street and west by Windsor et, is absolutely devastated.

THE wounded and homeless are in different institutions and homes over the city. The Halifax Herald is collecting information regarding the missing, and citizens who have victims of the disaster at their homes are requested to telephone to The Herald office. Hundreds of the bodies which were taken from the ruins are unrecognizable and morgues have been opened in different parts of the city. Citizens' committees are being formed for rescue work. Bulletins will be issued thruout the day giving information for the assistance of those who have lost relatives and friends. While practically every home in the city is damaged, those who are able to give any temporary accommodation are asked to notify some of the committees.

Military and naval patrols are keeping order and superintending the rescue work

AWFUL STORY OF DISASTER

9.05 o'clock yesterday morning a terrific explosion wrecked ax killing over a thousand, ding at least five thousand, and g in ruins at least one-fifth of ity.

The Belgian Relief steamer Imo ng down out of the Basin in ge of Pilot William Hayes collidth the French steamship Mont c in charge of Pilot Frank Mac-

The French steamer was loaded nitro glycerine and trinitrotuol. broke out on the Mont Blanc he was headed in for Pier 8. It eighteen minutes after the colwhen the explosion occurred. old sugar refinery, and all the

buildings for a great distance collapsed. Tug boats and steamers were engulfed and then a great wave rushed over Campbell road carrying up debris and the corpses of hundreds of men who were at work on the piers and steamers.

Without the loss of a moment hundreds of survivors rushed to the rescue of those buried in the ruins. Fire broke out in scores of places and soon the great mass of wreckage was in the grip of an uncontrollable fire checking the work of rescue.

The military and naval authorities almost immediately took charge of the situation. Fearing that the fire would reach local magazines of explosives military messengers were sent over the city warning the people

out of the buildings and advising them to take to the citadel and open spaces. This was not by authority.

Practically every house in the city was damaged. The entire business district was windowless and to prevent pillaging patrols from warships in port were paraded thru the streets.

All along Gottingen street and throughout the northwest part of the city there was a pitiful scene as women and children lacerated with flying fragments of glass rushed from their homes. Truckmen, hackmen, and taxi-cab drivers rushed victims to the hospitals for dressing. At the Naval hospital many of the sick sailors were badly cut and, fearing an explosion from the magazine at the Wellington barracks, they were taken away.

THE home of The Halifax Herald and The Evening Mail is badly wrecked. Every pane of glass and window in the building is smashed. Partitions have been blown down. Our press is filled with glass. Some employees have lost their homes and families. Our power service is cut off.

We are sending out a copy of this hand printed bulletin to every town in order that as many of our readers as possible may know at least some of the details of the disaster. We hope to be in a position to publish tomorrow. In the meantime we ask for patience.

A public meeting is called for city hall at 11.

Congress, called Flavelle "a great big hypocrite." Newspapers referred to "His Lardship" and the "Bacon Baron." Flavelle's example helped persuade Parliament in 1918 to abolish hereditary titles for Canadians.

The Growth of Government

In 1915, Borden had promised Parliament that his policy was "not to interfere with the business activities of the country." He believed deeply that Canadians could be trusted to do their duty as sincerely as he would himself. It had seemed natural to hand over key functions of the war effort to committees of businessmen and to civic leaders. Steadily, however, the government had been compelled to intervene.

After 1916, the Canadian Patriotic Fund continued to hand out money and a lot of advice to the families of soldiers overseas, but its funds now came directly from the government, not from generous citizens. The Military Hospitals Commission, run by Sir James Lougheed, an Alberta senator, met only twice as it grew from nothing to an organization with 78 institutions, 17,944 beds and a range of functions from making artificial arms to training chicken farmers. In 1918, much of its work was taken over by the army medical corps and a new Department of Soldiers' Civil Reestablishment.

Children stagger home under loads of coal. One of the familiar chores of children from poorer homes was to hunt for scattered lumps of coal. By 1917, fuel was scarce and costly, and such scavenging became even more vital to family welfare.

In many cases, it was the public, through newspaper editors and politicians, that demanded action. It was the government that responded, often with obvious reluctance. In November 1916, answering complaints of profiteering, the government solemnly asked companies not to horde supplies, raise prices or limit competition. It was like sitting on the sprinkler, complained one critic, instead of turning off the tap.

The fuel and food shortages in 1917 brought at least the appearance of tougher action. A new Fuel Controller, C. A. Magrath, had the power to jail coal dealers who hoarded stocks. Magrath decided who got scarce supplies, ordered fuelless days and negotiated with the Americans for a continuing share of their production. A Director of Coal Operations had the power to force both mine-owners and militant miners to keep producing on pain of fines or jail sentences.

The Food Controller approached his job very differently. W. J. Hanna had been head of Imperial Oil. Instead of rolling back prices, as people had hoped, Hanna told them to eat less and change their tastes. His Food Board got busy with a "Keep a Hog" campaign. It sold a thousand tractors to farmers at cost. A "Sea Food Special" brought fresh fish to Quebec and Ontario, and the Board persuaded butcher shops to buy fish display counters at half-price. Grocers and restaurant owners were deluged with regulations. By the summer of 1918, loyal Canadians were on their honour to limit themselves to a pound and a half of sugar per person per month. By October, butter was restricted to two pounds per person a month and "war bread" was sold with 20 percent of the flour replaced by substitutes.

Popular outrage against profiteering and demands to "conscript wealth" pushed a reluctant finance minister to change his ideas. In 1916, Sir Thomas White's budget included a tax on business profits that brought in $12.5 million. In April 1917, White insisted that there would be no income tax; the debate on the Military Service Act forced him to change his mind. On July 25, White finally announced that, for the period of the war only, a tax would be raised on corporate profits and personal incomes over $1500 for single people and over $3000 for families. The tax was a light burden for a small minority. The prime minister, one of only 31,130 Canadians who paid income tax in 1918, would have been taxed about $80 on his official salary.

The war also influenced the way the government treated the two badly troubled transcontinental railways. It affected the companies too. Without it, the Grand Trunk and the Canadian Northern might possibly have found new investors. Because of the crisis, the government had to keep every line in operation. Many people, and certainly Sir Thomas White, would have preferred to let one or both companies go into bankruptcy as a warning to foolish

BEEF AND BACON ON 5 DAYS ONLY

Public Eating Places Cannot Serve These Meats on Tuesdays and Fridays.

AT ONE MEAL ON OTHER DAYS

Definite Restrictions Placed on Certain Foods by Order-in-Council.

Ottawa, Aug. 9.—Definite regulations, to come into effect at once, for restricting the use of beef, bacon and white bread in public eating places, and for prohibiting the use of wheat in the distillation or manufacture of alcohol have been promulgated by order-in-Council at the instance of the Food Controller. The serving of beef and bacon is prohibited on Tuesdays and Fridays, and at more than one meal on any other day. Substitutes, such as corn bread, oatcake, potatoes, etc., must be provided at every meal at which white bread is served. Under the order the expression "bacon" includes cured (either pickled or smoked) sides, backs, hams and any portion of what is termed, in the trade, Wiltshire sides.

The term "public eating places" includes any hotel, restaurant, cafe—

Concluded on Page 2, Col. Two.

Toronto *Mail and Empire*, August 9, 1918.

speculators. The government as a whole believed that that was impossible. The old argument that Canada's credit rating would be affected was more serious when the government's borrowing in New York helped pay for the war effort. More quietly, Borden was never allowed to forget that the Bank of Commerce, his ally in the 1911 election, would lose heavily if Mackenzie and Mann went under.

In 1916, well aware that both Liberals and Conservatives would condemn official aid to the two lines, the government managed to pad its war estimates with $8 million for the Grand Trunk and $15 million for the Canadian Northern. Next, Borden sought advice from a Royal Commission. When it reported in 1917, the Commission confirmed most of what Borden himself had been saying since 1904. The Canadian Northern was broke and the Canadian public, which had paid 60 percent of its costs, should take it over. The only real problem, fought out through the courts and in Parliament during the hectic summer of 1917, was how much could be saved for the Bank of Commerce.

To Borden, there was still a painful irony in the fact that he was taking the abuse for mistakes committed by Laurier and his Liberals. A coalition with Laurier that summer would certainly have eased the railway question. The Union government was the next best thing. On December 20, three days after the election, the government created the Canadian National Railway. Merging the Canadian Northern, the National Transcontinental and the old Intercolonial Railway finally gave Canada a publicly-owned railway system that ran, sometimes very badly, from Vancouver to Halifax. The Grand Trunk and its Pacific extension would have to wait for two more years.

Before the war, Canadians consumed an average of 18 kilograms of fish per person per year. As a result of the government's efforts, consumption rose to 56.7 kilograms by 1917.

A New Government

Canada's thirteenth Parliament met for the first time on March 18, 1918, not in the old buildings, which had burned to the ground in February, 1916, but among the fossils and dinosaur skeletons in the National Museum. The jokes were obvious, but the new government had much to report. Election pledges of voting rights for all women, total prohibition of liquor and drastic reform of civil service hiring and promotion had all to be turned into law.

For the women who had campaigned so long for the right to vote, the final victory on May 24, 1918, was a tarnished triumph. As in Britain, it was offered as a reward for wartime services and sacrifices, but it had also become inevitable. In the prairie provinces, suffrage had come in 1916 largely because farm organizations and women themselves had made unanswerable arguments for equality. British Columbia had followed in 1917 and so had Ontario. On the war, the women's movement had again divided. Some, like Flora Denison and Francis Benyon, had joined the small, brave minority of pacifists; most had joined wholeheartedly in the struggle. Prohibition of liquor, always a cause closely linked with the women's cause, had triumphed in a wartime Canada committed to sacrifice and moral purification. Votes for women, prohibitionists argued, would consolidate the triumph of moral and social reform. Over furious objections from Quebec M.P.'s, who insisted that votes for women contradicted the laws of religion, history and biology, overdue justice was finally done. After a further struggle, in July 1919 women also won the right to hold federal office.

Now that the United States was in the war, Canada's relations with Washington had become far more important. Borden, who had spent a week in Virginia recuperating from the election campaign, came home by way of the American capital, visited President Woodrow Wilson and found that old differences had vanished. In 1911, he had won his election in a campaign that shrieked "No truck nor trade with the Yankees." Now he rejoiced that: "The Americans expressed the view that the resources of the two countries should be pooled in the most effective cooperation and that the boundary line had little or no significance in considering or dealing with these vital questions."

Soon, if Resolution IX meant anything, Canada would have her own embassy in Washington. Meanwhile, a Canadian War Mission under the energetic Lloyd Harris, would do just as well. In Ottawa, a War Trade Board was formed to work with the powerful War Industries Board in the United States, managing imports, exports and problems of scarcity.

Finding Soldiers

The new government's biggest job and the reason it existed was to find men for the Canadian Corps. By early January, it was obvious that the Military Service Act was a failure. Devised by the ingenious Arthur Meighen, it was really a law about exemptions, appeals and more appeals. While all men could be asked to serve, they or their lawyers had little trouble finding some excuse among the vague grounds for exemption, which ranged from family hardship to conscientious objection. Across Canada, members of 1239 tribunals were nominated equally by the government and the opposition. Their decisions could be questioned by 195 appeal courts and then by a central appeal judge, Mr. Lyman Duff of the Supreme Court of Canada.

Though critics called the law oppressive, a British historian was closer to the mark when he wrote that it "contained so many safeguards against oppression that it had been made in no small degree inoperative." It was certainly unpredictable. Ontario tribunals exempted Mennonites as conscientious objectors but not Jehovah's Witnesses. A ruling declared that Protestant theological students could be conscripted but not Catholic novices. Local opinions naturally influenced the tribunals. In Quebec, Duff later

Daylight Saving Time
Daylight saving time was first introduced in Canada in 1918 as a measure to conserve electricity.

"Soldiers of the Soil"
During the war, 11,952 boys between the ages of 15 and 19 registered as "Soldiers of the Soil" to help out on farms.

General Lessard

General Lessard was a permanent force cavalry officer, born in Quebec in 1860 and too old for the war. He had commanded a Canadian cavalry regiment in South Africa in 1900. After the war, he preferred to retire to Ontario and he died in Meadowvale, west of Toronto, in 1927.

claimed, the tribunals exempted almost every French-speaking applicant but "they applied conscription against the English-speaking minority in Quebec with a rigor unparalleled."

On January 3, when the first conscripts were called for training, only 20,000 reported. Many who failed to win exemptions simply disappeared. The small federal police forces had the thankless job of finding them. In Quebec, where people bitterly resented conscription, a clash was almost inevitable.

It came on the Easter week-end in Quebec City. Military police seized a young man who had no papers. Angry crowds attacked the military service registry office and threw the records into the snow. Then they roamed the streets, smashing the windows of English-owned businesses. Local police did nothing. When the local military commander appealed for help, Ottawa sent its senior French-Canadian officer, Major-General François Lessard, and 700 soldiers from Ontario. Rioting continued. At night on Easter Monday, some soldiers were surrounded on a square. Pelted with ice and bricks, they opened fire. Four civilians died, many were injured and the riots ended.

The violence shocked everyone. The Quebec clergy commanded faithful Catholics to obey the law. Ottawa took sweeping power to stop violence and promised to conscript anyone who interfered with enforcement of the Military Service Act. Quebeckers settled down to wait for political revenge.

Meanwhile, Canada and her allies faced a new and frightening threat. On March 21, 1918, a week before the Quebec riots, the German armies struck. Their target was the Fifth British Army, still recovering from Passchendaele. The German tactics were those of Cambrai — a heavy artillery bombardment, deep thrusts by tough, specially trained "stormtroops" hidden by smoke screens and fog. British strong points were bypassed, isolated and destroyed at leisure. In less than a week the Fifth Army had ceased to exist. It was a disaster without precedent, and it was repeated again and again that spring as German attacks drove the French and British from some of the most bloodstained ground on the Western Front.

In France, allied generals reacted desperately to the enemy thrusts. At Doullens on March 26, Field Marshal Sir Douglas Haig finally put his armies under the French commander, Marshal Ferdinand Foch. In the crisis, Borden's course was clear. Despite the political risks, men must be found. The farce of the Military Service Act must end. After a bitter cabinet debate, all exemptions were cancelled on April 12.

The risks for the government were real. Thomas Crerar, a Manitoba Liberal and president of the Grain Grower's Grain Company, had been a great asset to the Union government in Octo-

ber when he agreed to be minister of agriculture. Now he fought for his farmer constituents. In the parliamentary debate, the Unionist majority fell from seventy-one to only forty-three. Robbed of their sons and labourers, farmers completed their spring seeding as best they could and, on May 15, five thousand of them invaded Ottawa. The prime minister listened politely but ignored their appeals. Surely the war crisis mattered more than an election promise. Newspapers sneered at the "hayseed profiteers." The farmers went home seething with rage.

Some historians claim that not only was conscription a broken promise, it was also a miserable failure. They point out that only 24,100 conscripts actually fought in France. These historians play the old game of being wise after the event. No one anywhere expected in 1914 that the war would last four and a half years or that it would kill millions. And no one in 1917 could have believed that the war would end within a year. The Military Service Act was designed to find 100,000 soldiers. At the end of the war, 99,561 MSA men wore the uniform of the Canadian Expeditionary Force. If the war had continued into 1919, as almost

Men of the 22nd Battalion wait for the order to advance. The "Vandoos," the only French-Canadian unit in the Corps, won a superb reputation during the Somme offensives and again during the "Last Hundred Days." In one battle, every officer was killed or wounded.

everyone expected, those men would have been needed. Of course, the Act would never have worked if Borden had not cut out most of the exemptions.

Borden goes overseas

Sir Robert Borden and some of his key ministers were worn out by 1918. Sir Thomas White, Borden's closest friend in the government, insisted that he must resign or die an early death. By creating a coalition, Borden had hoped to end the tiresome squabbles over patronage and petty ambitions. Instead, some of his ministers carried on their old battles, determined to be in a good position when traditional party loyalties revived. Newton Rowell had promised his fellow Liberals that he would clean up past corruption and mismanagement. It seemed hard for him to understand that the people he attacked were now close colleagues and allies. Always the disputes came back to Borden, the man who had created the Unionist coalition. No one else was quite as trusted.

Borden had a very different view of his role. If Canada was to have a voice in the Empire's policy of making war and peace, only the prime minister could be that voice, and only by being in London would that voice be heard. As soon as he could possibly escape, he would rejoin the Imperial War Cabinet in London. This was the way to give meaning to the vague but exciting promises in Resolution IX.

First, of course, Borden must make sure that his country would not fall apart. On January 17, J. N. Francoeur, a Liberal, led a debate in the Quebec assembly that expressed the bitterness of French Canada. Yet, as Borden realized, Francoeur's resolution argued only that Quebec would leave Confederation if "in the view of the other provinces, it is believed that she is an obstacle to the union, progress and development of Canada." And, despite the grievances about imperialism, immigration and conscription, not a single Quebec member had spoken for separation. No one, Borden noted, had spoken more eloquently for Confederation than the premier, Sir Lomer Gouin.

Quebec, the prime minister advised, "should be left alone for the present." When he cancelled exemptions in April, he repeatedly emphasized that single men would be taken so that married men could stay home. That was an olive branch to Quebec. Finally, in May, Borden and Lomer Gouin met for dinner and a surprisingly easy conversation. From now on, Borden explained, the Quebec premier would control the handing out of federal jobs and contracts in his province. The Quebec leader did not need to be told his side of the bargain: Quebec would be quiet for the rest of the war.

Then, Borden was off across the Atlantic. There was much for him to learn.

Sir Thomas White
Despite his fears for his health, Sir Thomas White survived to 1955. Trained as a lawyer, he had been president of the National Trust Co. In the postwar years, he recorded the history of Canada's wartime finances and wrote two volumes of poetry.

Perhaps the most cheering fact was that the Canadian Corps had missed the brunt of the German attacks. Strung out along Vimy Ridge in a wider and wider front, as other troops were sent to plug the gaps, Currie's divisions had escaped the pulverising, demoralizing offensives. Currie had a confident explanation for the prime minister when they met. While Canadians had spent every ounce of energy adding barbed wire and improving defences, he claimed, British generals had ordered men to build tennis courts. Currie's contempt for his fellow commanders had burst out during the crisis, when Haig had sent some of the Canadians divisions to stem the German tide. The Canadian commander had insisted that his men be returned for they would fight better in the Corps than under any other command. Haig grumbled about Currie's swollen head, but the divisions came back.

Currie had won a battle with his Canadian superiors as well. By reorganizing the Corps, the government suggested, Canada could put six smaller divisions in the field and give itself two corps and an army headquarters. That would mean jobs for hundreds of the surplus officers in England, a wealth of promotions and, above all, a chance for Sam Hughes's son to command a division in France. To the government's amazement, Currie denounced the idea. The Corps, with its four divisions, had become a superb instrument. Additional staff officers would be untrained and incompetent. Perhaps above all, he had no room for Garnet Hughes. Currie's arguments worked.

There was an ironic aftermath. The 5th Division could no longer be justified in England. At last its battalions were broken up and more than twenty thousand reinforcements were suddenly available for the Corps. Without conscription, certainly without the cancellation of exemptions, the Canadian Corps had enough volunteers to carry it through the summer of 1918.

No one could have known that, least of all Sir Robert Borden. What he did know, when he went to Britain in May, was that he had met his responsibilities to the Imperial War Cabinet. He had gone home from the previous meeting and, at enormous cost, he had found the men needed to continue the war. Had the British kept their part of the bargain? Had they told the colonial leaders that Australians, New Zealanders and Canadians would be dragged through the mud of a Flanders offensive? After Currie met his prime minister and told him more about the terrible struggle at Passchendaele and his own version of the March disasters, Borden was close to the boiling point. "Mr. Prime Minister," he told Lloyd George, "I want to tell you that if there is a repetition of the battle of Passchendaele, not a Canadian soldier will leave the shores of Canada so long as the Canadian people entrust the government of their country to my hands."

Chances are that the British prime minister was pleased.

Sir Arthur Currie
While British generals received titles and large cash rewards for their services, Sir Arthur Currie gained no honours for his overseas service. The government dared not defy strong public opposition to any special treatment for generals. The former school teacher and insurance agent was, however, chosen as principal of McGill University in 1920 and he held the position until his death in 1933.

Lloyd George's own contempt for British generalship was now limitless, and he made sure that senior commanders had to listen in person to Borden's words. Then he invited a committee of dominion prime ministers to work with the generals in looking at the past and future conduct of the war. Borden worked hard in the committee, but its report was unfinished and unsigned when he went back to Canada on August 16. In its incomplete form, the report argued that the British army should stay on the defensive in 1919, building its strength for a decisive blow in 1920. Meanwhile, a major effort must be made to topple the Bolshevik regime and get the Russians back in the war against Germany.

With that policy in mind, Borden could not refuse British requests for Canadian artillery to join an expedition to Archangel in the Russian Arctic and for a Canadian brigade to occupy the terminus of the Trans-Siberian railway at Vladivostok. What troops were more naturally suited to the long Russian winter than Canadians?

Even as they were landing in their strange, remote theatres of war, events had acquired their own momentum on the Western Front. Borden and his fellow politicians proved no better than generals in predicting history.

Canada's "Hundred Days"

Sir Douglas Haig knew his orders: there would be no more big offensives. Instead, he must push the Germans back from some of their spring gains around the vital railway town of Amiens. The Canadians and the Australians, nine divisions in all, would be backed by 2000 guns and 470 tanks. Instead of the long, leisurely bombardment of previous offensives, the attack would come as a surprise. The Canadians, obviously now the strongest single element among the British armies in the field, secretly moved north to their new battle. Now that wireless was part of an army's equipment, special units broadcast floods of messages to convince the Germans that the Corps was still in its old positions. To hide the noise of moving tanks hundreds of aircraft roared overhead. At dawn on August 8, preparations ended and the battle began.

Amiens was the triumph the generals had waited for. Only one Canadian division, the 4th, was caught by heavy machine gun fire. The tanks, far better armed and more reliable than at their introduction two years before, finally worked out their partnership with infantry. Aircraft, in new tactics, zoomed down on German trenches, blasting them with bombs. Like the Germans, the Canadians had stopped attacking in line. Instead, platoons and companies went forward as small teams, by-passing the toughest German resistance. In a single day, the Canadians went forward thirteen kilometres and the Australians on their left went almost as far. The Corps lost 1036 dead and 2803 wounded, but the German

Right: Victims of mustard gas in an ambulance. Chlorine gas, released on Canadians in 1915, was succeeded by even more horrible agents like mustard gas, which burned skin and breathing passages. Victims suffered agonies. Below: A tank waits to advance as stretcher bearers bring back a casualty.

HUMAN COST OF THE WAR

	Total Force Mobilized	Military Deaths	Military Wounded	Civilian Deaths
Allies				
France	8,410,000	1,357,800	4,266,000	40,000
British Empire	8,904,467	908,371	2,090,212	30,633
(Canada)	(619,636)	(60,661)	(144,606)	*
Russia	12,000,000	1,700,000	4,950,000	2,000,000
Italy	5,615,000	462,391	953,886	*
United States	4,355,000	50,585	205,690	*
Belgium	267,000	13,715	44,686	30,000
Serbia	707,343	45,000	133,148	650,000
Montenegro	50,000	3,000	10,000	*
Roumania	750,000	335,706	120,000	275,000
Greece	230,000	5,000	21,000	132,000
Portugal	100,000	7,222	13,751	*
Japan	800,000	300	907	*
Total	42,188,810	4,888,891	12,809,280	3,157,633
Central Powers				
Germany	11,000,000	1,808,546	4,247,143	760,000
Austria-Hungary	7,800,000	922,500	3,620,000	300,000
Turkey	2,850,000	325,000	400,000	2,150,000
Bulgaria	1,200,000	75,844	152,390	275,000
Total	22,850,000	3,131,889	8,419,533	3,485,000
Grand total	65,038,810	8,020,780	21,228,813	6,642,633

* Figures not available   SOURCE: *Academic American Encyclopedia*

Many of these figures are approximations as official figures are not always available and sometimes contradict each other. Canadian totals, although shown, are included in those of the British Empire.

front-line divisions had ceased to exist. The Canadians took 5033 prisoners and 161 guns.

The German chief of staff, General Erich von Ludendorff, called Amiens "the black day of the German army in the history of this war." The losses could never be replaced and the number of prisoners, two-thirds of the casualties, showed that German morale had finally begun to crack.

It was far from gone, though, and by August 9, the advance ran out of steam. Currie had learned a lesson: stop while you are ahead. On August 11, when the Corps stopped attacking, it faced troops from eighteen German divisions. The answer was to change fronts. Haig agreed and he also insisted to his British political superiors that the war might be won not in 1920 but in a matter of months.

It seemed hard to believe. The British now faced the German Hindenberg Line, a line of trenches and fortifications that had taken two years to build. It was easily the toughest obstacle Canadians would face. Once again, Currie's secret was patience, preparation and masses of carefully-aimed artillery fire. There was no easy way to do it. Breaking through the first German line cost the two attacking divisions almost six thousand men. Every officer of the 22nd Battalion including a future governor general, Major Georges Vanier, was killed or wounded. After almost a week's rest, the Corps attacked the Drocourt-Quéant line. It was even stronger and better prepared but the Canadians broke through. The assault cost six thousand dead or wounded, but after two days it was the Germans who withdrew.

One major obstacle remained; the unfinished Canal du Nord. Once again, Currie insisted on time to prepare. His battered divisions rested and absorbed the first big drafts of conscripts. When the Corps went forward again on September 26, Currie had adopted his own risky strategy. He would drive across the canal on a narrow front, create a bridgehead and pour his divisions through the gap. It was a test of planning, efficiency and the fighting spirit of the leading attackers. Once again, the Corps broke through. Then, for more than a week, the Canadians fought their way toward Cambrai. By October 11, the town had fallen.

In forty-seven days of almost steady fighting, the Canadians had been in the spearhead of the British army. The price was heavy, 30,802 dead and wounded, and the gains may now seem meagre — 18,585 German prisoners, 371 guns, 2000 machine guns and 300 square kilometres of French territory. Yet the Canadians were ending the war in battles which destroyed the German army. The Germans did not crumble — they were far too disciplined soldiers for that — but they fell back and the Canadians led the pursuit.

This was the open phase of war of which the generals had dreamed and for which the armies of trench warfare were now unprepared. Now came the exhaustion of long marches and real hunger when the horse-drawn wagons and cookers failed to keep up. German troops fought tough, costly rearguard battles. The war zone was now far behind, and heavy fighting or artillery barrages would kill more French civilians than Germans. When Germans held the industrial city of Valenciennes, the Canadians were forced to work their way around it to avoid hurting the population. The operation was a success. The Germans, trying to break out, lost 2400 dead and prisoners; 80 Canadians died.

Now the Canadians could move forward, soaked by the steady November rains but almost unopposed as they crossed the Belgian border and approached the town of Mons, where the war had begun for the British Expeditionary Force in August 1914. Now it was the Germans who would stand and fight behind canals and fortified houses. All day on November 10, soldiers of the Royal Canadian Regiment and the 42nd Highlanders from Montreal fought their way through the suburbs of the town. By daybreak on the eleventh the enemy had fled or been destroyed. At 9 A.M., the message finally reached the front lines. At 11 A.M., firing would cease. The war was over.

Kaiser Wilhelm II
In late October and early November, revolts flared in Germany. Kaiser Wilhelm II abdicated on November 9 and fled next day to the Netherlands, where he lived quietly as a country gentleman until his death in 1941.

Waiting for peace

Across Canada that summer and fall, there had been none of the excitement that had sent men of the Corps into battle with the hope of an early release. The war had lasted too long for that. In its final year, there was a grim, repressive mood in the country. Labour mourned the killing of one of its leaders, Albert Goodwin, shot by police as he avoided arrest as a draft-dodger. Catholics and Protestants traded abuse after military police were sent on a midnight raid on the Jesuit novitiate at Guelph.

An "anti-loafing law" threatened jail or fines for men and even boys who could not prove that they were fully employed. The government succumbed to the pressure of C. H. Cahan, a Montreal lawyer, to make him head of national security. For the first time, police spies were sent to watch labour and political meetings. Both federal police organizations, the Dominion Police in the East and the Royal North-West Mounted Police in the West, recruited informers and began spying on ordinary Canadians. Their findings, incidentally, were reassuring: people were fed up, but really radical talk was almost non-existent. Canadians simply wanted to get the war over.

Urged by Cahan and local patriots, the government reluctantly banned a number of labour and radical organizations. Newspapers in "enemy" languages were outlawed unless they could get a special licence and promise to reprint every word in English. Veterans organizations, backed by the Orange lodge and provincial politicians demanded immediate mass internment of all enemy aliens. Government ministers could only protest that international law forbade such a procedure.

Influenza
The death toll world-wide of the 1918 influenza epidemic is estimated to have reached between ten and twenty million.

The grim mood of Canadians in 1918 had an additional explanation. A world-wide influenza epidemic that year probably took more lives than the entire war. In early September, the first cases were reported in the United States. Days later, it reached Quebec and Ontario. By the end of the year, one Canadian in six had been affected. Schools were closed for weeks, factories shut down, and railway, telephone and postal services were crippled for lack of workers. In some small communities, almost everyone was stricken and there was no one to nurse sick and helpless people.

The war had taught Canadians to look to governments in crisis, but no level of authority in Canada had either direct responsibility or the means to help in a health crisis. As the extent of the epidemic slowly was appreciated, Ottawa, the provinces and municipalities struggled to respond. Schools, hotels, even provincial legislatures became makeshift hospitals. Women volunteered as "Sisters of Service" to help in smaller communities. Often they became victims because the virus killed men and women in the prime of life as quickly as the elderly and the young. No final death toll could ever be established but between 30,000 and 50,000 Canadians died from the epidemic before the end of 1918.

On November 9, at its height, a strange hysteria suddenly sent Canadians into the streets to cheer the end of the war. No one yet knows how the rumours of the "false armistice" began but the let-down in its wake was only temporary. Early on November 11, morning newspapers carried the news. The fighting had ended. The men could come home.

REVIEW AND DISCUSSION

Key People and Ideas
Explain the importance of each of the following people and ideas as they are discussed in the chapter.

W. F. O'Connor   The Halifax Explosion
David Lloyd George   The Canadian National Railway
Woodrow Wilson   The Hindenberg Line
Thomas Crerar   The Imperial War Cabinet
Sir Lomer Gouin

Analysing the Issues
Answer each of the following questions, which deal with important issues raised in the chapter.

— What factors led the finance minister to introduce taxes on corporate profits and personal incomes?
— What factors led to women receiving the vote in Canada on May 24, 1918?
— What were the key events in the final "Hundred Days" of the war?
— What factors led to the successes of the Canadian troops over these "Hundred Days"?

Questions for Discussion
Think carefully about each of the following questions and discuss the issues they raise.

— The arguments for "conscription of wealth" became widespread by 1917. Should the Borden government have intervened in the economy to ensure that businessmen and their companies could not make large profits from the war effort, or were the profits justified by the quality of service provided?
— What were the factors for and against Borden's decision, in April 1918, to cancel all exemptions under the Military Service Act? Did he make the proper decision?

6

DIVIDED NATION

The armistice found Canadian soldiers scattered from northern Scotland to the biblical lands of Mesopotamia. Four thousand had landed at Vladivostok, and at Baku on the Caspian Sea, a handful of Canadians were helping to organize a local army. For Canadian gunners at Archangel there was no cease-fire. They spent November 11 near Tulgas supporting American infantry in a desperate battle against the infant Red Army.

Sir Robert Borden was on the huge liner, *Mauretania*, on November 11. Two weeks before, Lloyd George had summoned him. The end of the war was in sight: if the Empire was to enter the peace conference as a unit, the dominion prime ministers must consult. Besides, the cautious Canadian might calm down William Hughes, the excitable Australian premier, who was demanding an independent role for his country at the conference.

Lloyd George misjudged his man. In answering the British invitation, Borden had warned: "The press and people of this country take it for granted that Canada will be represented at the Peace Conference." That did not mean, as Lloyd George soon found, a chance to take turns with India and other dominions in one of the five seats allotted to Britain.

Borden had moved a long way from the innocent imperialism of 1911 or the "Ready, Aye, Ready" spirit of 1914. He knew, for example, that Canada would never again allow itself to be at war simply because Britain had declared it. As surely as the Revolutionary War of 1776-83 had won American independence, the First World War would make Canada a sovereign nation. To Borden, that was the reward for the 60,661 dead and the terrible internal conflicts over conscription. The fact that Canada had been an ally, not an enemy, of those from whom she sought recognition made Canada's case even more unanswerable.

As the allied leaders gathered in Paris to dispose of their shattered and starving enemies and to shape a new Europe, Canada's concerns did not seem very important. Dozens of countries had joined the allies once their victory seemed inevitable. All were represented at the peace conference. The tall, bespectacled Woodrow Wilson, welcomed by cheering throngs, seemed to promise a new idealism and a respect for the rights of small nations. In fact, the postwar world would be fashioned by leaders of the three largest powers.

Wilson, with his professorial arrogance, was easily managed by a tough, cynical old Georges Clemenceau. Why, wondered the French premier, had Wilson needed fourteen points to describe his vision of a perfect world, when the good Lord had needed only ten commandments? Both men suspected their third partner, the wily Lloyd George. Pretending that colonies, dominions, call them what you will, were really independent countries was merely a British trick to get more influence. As a final concession, the do-

Opposite page: Special constables on the march during the Winnipeg General Strike in 1919. Having fired the city police for alleged pro-strike sympathies, the city council called on untrained but anti-strike civilians to help keep order. They were not a great success.

minions might each have one seat while sovereign nations like Portugal got two.

It was Lloyd George who felt the Canadian and Australian wrath. Borden raged that Canada had lost more dead than Portugal had sent troops to the war. His passion and Lloyd George's pressure finally worked. President Wilson, main opponent of the Canadian claim, finally gave way. Seats at the peace conference, he admitted, did not give extra votes.

What they did do was give status. The symbolic recognition gave Canada a claim to a bigger symbolic prize, a seat in the new League of Nations, the world organization created by the victors. Once again the Americans objected, insisting that the dominions were mere British puppets. Again, it was a weary President Wilson who gave way. Borden's quiet struggle for independence had taken a giant step forward. In the League and in its first big agency, the International Labour Organization, Canada would be as much a nation as any other.

The Group of Seven
Canada's most influential art movement, the Group of Seven, was formed in 1919 and held its first exhibition in Toronto in 1920. Tom Thompson, whose name is often associated with the group and who was a great influence on it, had drowned mysteriously in Northern Ontario in 1917.

Then and later, few Canadians understood Borden's preoccupation. What did it matter that Canada's own signature appeared on the peace treaty — even if it was below and slightly indented from that of Great Britain? And why had Borden insisted that Canada's Parliament debate and approve the peace treaty. It was, said W. S. Fielding, Laurier's old finance minister, "a colossal humbug." Other, more thoughtful critics argued that by joining the League Canada had lost independence, not gained it. Article X of the League's covenant, or constitution, made every member agree to defend the postwar boundaries though some of them were obviously unfair. Now Canada might have to go to war just because France or Italy or perhaps even Germany said so.

To that, Borden had no answer. He and other Canadians had opposed Article X, but it had been imposed by Clemenceau and the French. The League was imperfect. It was also the only hope of guaranteeing that the world really had fought the war to end all wars.

Neither Borden nor Woodrow Wilson could persuade his own people of the significance of the League. Canadians would grumble, maintain their membership and do their best to ignore the risks imposed by Article X. Their American neighbours rejected the League. Among the arguments hurled against Wilson was that he had let Britain's colonies have votes in the new organization. Americans still insisted in 1919 that Canada was no more than a dependency of the British Empire.

Governing Postwar Canada

For all his frustrations, Borden had enjoyed the long months in Paris. He was sick of cabinet squabbling and Canadian politics. He enjoyed the long confidential chats with Lloyd George, his

contacts with the great, even chores like working on a new Greek boundary. He relaxed, went to the theatre, even studied French.

In Ottawa, his ministers deplored his absence and pleaded for his return. The country was in turmoil. The shortages and problems of the war years continued and some got worse. Food and fuel were as scarce as ever. Worn-out railways delayed the return of Canada's 300,000 soldiers. Meanwhile, within days of the end of the war, the Imperial Munitions Board cancelled its contracts and 289,000 workers lost their jobs.

That would have mattered less if business and governments had worked out plans to create new jobs and opportunities. But that would have meant interference with business! Instead, Sir Thomas White, still finance minister as well as acting prime minister, insisted that government spending must be cut. The powerful chartered banks welcomed the peace by calling in loans, raising interest rates and sending the Canadian economy into a drastic depression. It was, of course, proper, orthodox economics. It was also an economic disaster from which everyone suffered — except the banks.

That was not what most Canadians had expected of the peace. They had looked forward to rewards for their sacrifices. In the biblical language that many people then appreciated, Canada

King St., Toronto, on Armistice Day, November 11, 1918. Across the country whistles blew, church bells rang and work stopped as thousands of laughing, cheering people thronged the streets to celebrate.

was to emerge from the fiery furnace of the war as a purified and perfected nation. A host of authors had tried to interest war-weary Canadians in new visions of their future. Salem Bland, a Winnipeg Methodist, wrote *A New Christianity*, arguing that religion must be an ally of social reform. Laurier's former minister of labour, William Lyon Mackenzie King, wrote *Industry and Humanity*, arguing that labour and management could work together to create a better society. Nellie McClung had won votes for women in Manitoba in 1916. Her book, *In Times Like These*, argued that women could now use their power to make a better, more pure world. "Humanity," she wrote, "can do anything it wants to do."

Nothing showed the radical impact of war on a conservative mind better than an essay by Stephen Leacock. The author of *Sunshine Sketches* had moved a long way when he concluded "The Unsolved Riddle of Social Justice" by writing: "Put in the plainest way, we are saying that the government of every country ought to supply work and pay to the unemployed, maintenance to the infirm and aged, and education and opportunity for the children."

That kind of society was a long way off in the Canada of 1919 but some people were thinking hard about it. In April, the government set up a Royal Commission on Industrial Relations to look at the cause and cure of labour unrest. Its report called for unemployment insurance, minimum wages, the eight-hour day and a law requiring employers and workers to bargain collectively. The problems of the influenza epidemic led to the creation of a federal Department of Health. For the first time, Ottawa offered money to the provinces for technical training, highways and housing.

Unemployment Insurance
An Unemployment Insurance Act was finally passed in 1940 and went into effect in 1942. The first effective collective bargaining legislation at the federal level was passed in 1944.

The wartime victory of women in winning the vote in federal elections and in most of the provinces had been associated with the triumph of prohibition. Both struggles continued in postwar Canada, particularly after the Senate voted down a law that would have continued the wartime ban on liquor into the postwar period. With strong support from women's organizations, all provinces but Quebec passed prohibition legislation, creating bitter controversies that lasted well into the twenties. In Nova Scotia, women had won the vote on April 26, 1918; in New Brunswick they had to wait until April 17, 1919. Prince Edward Island, small, rural and socially conservative, delayed until May 3, 1922, while Quebec, where conservatism and nationalism were allied in resisting an "Anglo-Saxon" notion, kept women from voting in provincial elections until 1940.

One way Canada showed she was a different country in 1919 was in her treatment of disabled soldiers. Veterans of earlier wars had often been left as cripples to beg on street corners. By 1920, Canadian war pension rates were the highest in the world. Government programmes promised to retrain disabled soldiers, help them find jobs and provide them with low-cost insurance. At the end of

1919, Canada was supporting 91,251 war pensioners, training 22,000 of them and treating about 8000 sick and injured veterans in hospital.

Even before the Armistice, J. W. Dafoe, editor of the Manitoba *Free Press*, predicted that anyone in government in the postwar period would have a thankless task. "It is going to be demanded of him that he do things which cannot be done; things which are mutually contradictory and destructive, and whatever he does will have more critics than friends." A good example was the government's attempt to control prices. When a special Cost of Living Commissioner suggested stiff laws against monopolies and profiteering, Arthur Meighen had an answer. In April 1919, a Board of Commerce was created with the power to look into and stop price increases. The board chairman, however, thought such powers were too dangerous, while one of the members, W. F. O'Connor, demanded drastic action. Public quarrelling by the two men made the Board useless.

Labour and the General Strike

The government's fiercest critic seemed to be organized labour. While British and American union leaders had become trusted wartime advisers of their governments, Canadian labour had had no voice in policy-making. Only in 1918 was Gideon Robertson, a very conservative unionist, appointed to be minister of labour. The Borden government had forbidden workers to go on strike, but it only "recommended" that employers pay fair wages and negotiate with their employees. Most of them paid no heed. Workers were told to make sacrifices for the war effort. They found out that a wealthy man like Sir Joseph Flavelle had earned $1,685,345 in just three wartime years.

Despite employer hostility, unions grew from 143,200 members in 1915 to 248,900 in 1918. With the war over, growth was even faster, to 378,000 men and women in 1919. Most of the new unionists worked in factories or as municipal employees. Even policemen joined unions. Few city councils or factory owners had ever faced unions before and they did not intend to start. There was no law that said how workers and employers could get together to settle disputes. If workers wanted their new unions to bargain for more pay to meet soaring living costs, there was only one way to do it: by striking. Never in Canadian history has more time been lost through strikes than in 1919.

If most employers wanted to crush unions, an angry minority of Western Canadian labour leaders wanted to overthrow the economic system. Often they were self-educated, articulate veterans of British and European socialist or labour parties. They were the men employers meant when they had put up signs saying "No English need apply".

Cost of Living
Experts who calculated what it should cost for food, rent, fuel, clothing and other basic needs claimed that a man who earned $28 a week in 1921 could provide the basic necessities for the average family of five.

Munition workers wait in the rain for their last pay cheque. Shutting munition factories when the war ended made sense, but soaring postwar interest rates did not. Bankers made profits, but few businessmen could afford loans to adjust to a peacetime market. The result was high unemployment.

In 1918 these men had gone home from the Trades and Labour Congress convention, determined that the West would have its own, more radical voice. They met again at Calgary in March 1919. In a few days of angry, excited speeches, the 239 delegates pledged support for a six-hour working day, sent greetings to revolutionaries in Russia and Germany and threatened a general strike. Then they hurried home to organize a new kind of union that would break with the old labour organizations in the East and the United States.

On May 15, the Winnipeg General Strike began. Within a day, almost thirty thousand workers had left their jobs. Canada's third largest city, the symbol of the booming West, was paralyzed.

The Winnipeg strike had nothing to do with the Calgary conference. A year before, a strike by all the city workers had forced a quick end to a dispute between the city council and its employees. Winnipeg labour leaders believed that the same tactics would make owners of three big factories in the city come to terms with their workers. Across Canada and even in Winnipeg, influential Canadians believed that the huge general strike spelled revolution. In Ottawa, Sir Thomas White had been so frightened by the Calgary meeting and by strikes in British Columbia that he wired Borden in Paris to ask that a British cruiser be sent to Vancouver. The Prime

Minister had snorted at the suggestion, but in Canada, the fears were real. Every day, newspapers reported Bolshevik massacres in Russia.

J. W. Dafoe's reaction was typical. Dafoe had been a reformer. He knew a little of the hardships workers faced in the slums of Winnipeg's North End. He knew that many Winnipeg employers were very rich and very stubborn. He knew that Winnipeg's labour leaders, even the most fiery speakers like Bob Russell, were basically sensible, moderate men, almost all of them of British or Canadian origin. Yet Dafoe reacted to the general strike with a fear and anger that blinded him to fact. Employees of the *Free Press* had joined the strike. Once he had re-opened the paper with non-union workers, Dafoe blasted the strikers as enemy aliens and revolutionaries. Convinced that this was the case, Arthur Meighen proposed changes to the Immigration Act that allowed naturalized citizens to be deported without trial if even suspected of trying to change society by force. This appalling law passed through Parliament in about twenty minutes.

By mid-June, the strike was failing. The strike committee had no funds and workers had few savings. Sympathetic strikes in cities across Canada had collapsed. Railway unions told members to go back to work or lose their pensions. Ottawa simply fired its striking postal workers. The collapse was not fast enough for Gideon Robertson, the labour minister, or for Meighen. Claiming that strike leaders had plotted to establish a Soviet-style regime, the government arrested ten of them before dawn on June 17. When strikers, veterans, women and children gathered on Winnipeg's Main Street on June 21 in a mass protest, the mayor called out troops. A squadron of Royal North-West Mounted Police charged into the crowd again and again. The third time, they fired revolvers. Special police, recruited from the city's middle class, flailed the crowd with baseball bats. Two died. Dozens were hurt.

In the striker's newspaper, J. S. Woodsworth, the former Methodist minister and pacifist, wrote about "Bloody Saturday." He was arrested. The strike ended on June 25. Two days later, Meighen moved amendments to the Criminal Code outlawing any organization which advocated change by force. Membership meant guilt "in the absence of proof to the contrary." The strike leaders were tried. Most were convicted and sentenced to a year in jail. Bob Russell, who had opposed the strike but who had been prominent at the Calgary meeting, got two years. Woodsworth, whose "sedition" included quoting passages from the Bible, was never tried.

At the time, the strike seemed to inspire more labour trouble than ever. The One Big Union, the organization Russell and the Calgary meeting had planned, spread across the West like wildfire after it was launched in June. Western unionists tore up their old

Strikes
In 1919, 0.5 percent of total working time was lost in strikes. Only in 1946 and 1976 has the strike record come close.

union cards. They soon found that the new organization could do nothing for them. As a weapon, the general strike was a failure. Within a year, organizers from the Trades and Labour Congress were busy trying to rebuild in the ruins of a labour movement. Employers warily made sure that they never succeeded. Only the bitterness remained. In Winnipeg's North End, it provided a safe haven for labour and socialist politics for half a century

The Farmers' Movement

It was not the Winnipeg General Strike that brought Sir Robert Borden hurrying home from Paris. It was the news that Thomas Crerar and the farmers were threatening to quit the government.

In 1910, the political power of western farmers had prodded Laurier into the reciprocity agreement and his political downfall. The political setback in 1911 and the wartime prosperity gave the farmers both a cause and a new confidence. A Council of Agriculture, founded in 1909, became a national voice for increasingly powerful provincial organizations in Ontario and the West. A Farmer's Platform in 1916 collected the familiar rural grievances — the tariff, freight rates, bank interest rates — and demanded action.

In 1917, the farm organizations had swung solidly behind the new Union government and, once they were assured of exemptions from the Military Service Act, so had farmers. Most of Borden's western members were Liberal Unionists elected by farm votes. Most of them feared that there would be no welcome back to their old party. Party roots on the prairies, shallow in the past, had vanished. In 1918, cancellation of exemptions had shaken Borden's rural M.P.s. Angry farmers had not been content to march on Ottawa; they had left behind a revised Farmers' Platform boldly termed "A New National Policy."

It was not very new and it certainly had nothing to do with John A. Macdonald. The Policy called for immediate cuts in the tariff and early elimination of any duties on farm machinery or the necessities of life. It wanted nationalized railways as well as continued and stiffer income, corporation and inheritance taxes. As a programme, it won prompt support from farmers in Ontario and all three prairie provinces.

The next question was how to make it happen. "We have grovelled and been ground in the dirt," claimed Alberta's Henry Wise Wood. "We are determined that this shall not be. We will organize for our protection; we will nourish ourselves and gain strength and then we shall strike out in our might and overthrow our enemies." This was a little vague. Wood and his followers had a strong if mystic faith that all virtue rested in the soil and those who worked it. The old politics of parties and deals was corrupt. Wood's theory of "Group Government" argued that Parliament

Between 1913 and the end of the war, there was an 80-percent increase in the amount of prairie land under cultivation.

Recall and Initiative
The New National Policy also called for some political reforms like the recall and the initiative that were meant to make Canada more democratic. The recall would allow voters to dismiss a representative who displeased them. The initiative would give voters a chance to propose laws and have them approved in a referendum. A number of American states have adopted one or both of these devices.

should be a meeting ground of interest groups like farmers, merchants and labour. By respecting each other, all would win.

On the prairies, where farmers seemed to be the only group in sight, Wood's theory might make sense, but most people had their doubts. It was also hard to change the political game without first using the rules to win. Crerar was more practical. In Borden's government, he had seen himself as the farmer representative. If the Union government wanted farmer support after the war, Crerar's terms were clear: it must adopt the New National Policy.

Amidst all the other crises of postwar Canada, Sir Thomas White and the Conservative members of the cabinet were now expected to abandon the high-tariff policies they had fought for in 1911. The government made a remarkable effort. Despite solemn wartime promises, the income and corporation taxes not only remained in White's new budget, they were dramatically increased. They had to be because the budget halved the tariff on many of the items on the farmers' list. Meanwhile the tireless Arthur Meighen promised to add the Grand Trunk and the Grand Trunk Pacific to Canada's nationalized railways. What more could Crerar want?

The answer, of course, was the whole programme. Canadian farmers were at a turning point and so was Canada. In 1891 and even in 1911, two-thirds of Canadians lived in villages or the countryside; in 1921, the census would find a slight majority of Canadians in cities and large towns. Canada's future would be urban and industrial, not rural and agricultural. This was the last moment for Canadian farmers to have political power and they knew it. The war had brought them political and economic gains. Prohibition of liquor was a rural blow against city immorality. So was the Lord's Day Act, clamping a puritanical Sunday on all Canadians. Wartime incomes allowed farmers to buy land, machinery and luxuries. Saskatchewan had become the second largest car-owning province thanks to wheat prices of two dollars a bushel. Yet the war had cost heavily too. Sons who had joined the army would stay in the cities to work. So would hundreds of thousands who had left rural Quebec and Ontario to work in Flavelle's factories. City-dwellers showed no sympathy as postwar farm prices collapsed, leaving farmers desperately short of cash to pay off wartime investments.

In theory and sometimes in practice, farmers and labour could be allies. From both groups, leaders denounced traditional politics and parties and spoke of a new social order. Both raged at "greedy bankers" and "bloated capitalists." Political alliances seemed easy since farmers could run in rural constituencies while labour candidates ran in the cities. In practice, the differences were sharp. Most farmers opposed the idea of governments helping the poor or the unemployed. They were appalled by shorter working hours. Farmers were not socialists, only very small capitalists!

Population – 1911

Montreal	*470,480*
Toronto	*376,538*
Winnipeg	*136,035*
Vancouver	*100,401*
Ottawa	*87,062*
Hamilton	*81,969*
Quebec	*78,190*
London	*46,300*
Calgary	*43,704*
Edmonton	*24,900*

Population – 1921

Montreal	*618,506*
Toronto	*521,893*
Winnipeg	*179,087*
Vancouver	*117,217*
Hamilton	*114,151*
Ottawa	*107,843*
Quebec	*95,193*
Calgary	*63,305*
London	*60,959*
Edmonton	*58,821*

Two-Party System
Since Liberals and Conservatives had monopolized Canadian politics since 1854, any interloper was automatically dismissed as a "third party." In fact, Ontario had first elected a strong contingent of farmers in 1894, and the first Labour member won a seat in Parliament in 1887. By 1921, the two-party system was obsolete in Canada, though Liberals and Conservatives hated to admit it.

Station XWA (now CFCF) in Montreal transmitted the first scheduled radio broadcast in North America on May 20, 1920.

In October 1919, the Ontario Conservative government, went down to stunning defeat. The astonished winners, the United Farmers of Ontario, had not even chosen a leader. When Ernest Drury, a Simcoe County farmer, became premier, he first had to find himself a seat. With his forty-three seats and eleven from labour, Drury gave Ontario its first third-party government. Others followed in Manitoba in 1920, when several of the jailed strike leaders gained seats, and in Alberta, where the United Farmers and a handful of labour members had a brief trial of Wood's theories of "group government."

Whatever the form, the farmers were finally in politics on their own. In June 1919 Crerar left the Union cabinet. Farmer candidates won four by-elections that year, in three different provinces. On February 26, 1920, Crerar and ten other members of Parliament met with the Canadian Council of Agriculture and announced that they would sit as the National Progressive Party. Purists among the farmers, like Wood, grumbled that it was all dangerously like political partyism, but the farmers now had a political focus and Canada had her first real third party.

Businessmen and Railways

Of all the storms that came roaring out of the West in 1919, one alarmed the government even more than farmers or labour. Veterans, pouring back to Canada from the wet, ill-managed Canadian camps in England and France, expected a hero's welcome. They found, for the most part, that Canadians had learned to live without them. Government generosity was reserved for the disabled and for dependents of the war-dead; the able-bodied must fend for themselves. Even those who found jobs abandoned them with a restlessness few could explain. Suddenly, the veterans, too, found a focus. A meeting at Calgary on a cold Sunday in February offered a simple answer to the grievances of 300,000 men. In 1917, Borden had promised soldiers "full re-establishment." The government could provide it with a bonus of $2000 for each man who had served in France, a little less for those who had stayed in England or Canada.

The bonus campaign raced across Canada, backed by patriots, municipal councils, women's organizations and by politicians delighted to embarrass the government. The Liberals, meeting for their leadership convention, endorsed the bonus demand. Borden's government refused. Paying the bonus would cost just under a billion dollars, half the national debt. Once again, the Union government was caught in a swirl of anger and discontent. It held firm. Bluntly, the government warned the House of Commons that if it wanted the bonus, it could find a new cabinet. Most M.P.'s, nervously aware that they faced defeat, backed the government they had. Canada's returned soldiers discovered that their

influence faded fast. One sad side-effect was a quiet government decision to tighten up on pensions and benefits for the disabled. Normality was returning.

For Canadian businessmen, it was none too soon. Industrialists and financiers had been national heroes in the Laurier boom and the early war years; now they found themselves hated, feared and under attack. Farmers and labour found common ground in denouncing eastern capitalists. Angry veterans made no secret of where they would find the money for their bonus. Yet, far from seeing Borden's battered government as their defender, businessmen were just as angry at its policies and as impatient at its compromises as were the clamorous farmers, workers and veterans. White's compromise on the tariff not only failed to pacify farmers; it enraged industrialists.

Between them, White and Meighen tackled the final stage of their long, tiresome struggle with the transcontinentals. In the circumstances, the Grand Trunk management badly needed a favour. Despite another $7.5 million in 1917, the company was too deep in debt to recover. If the government could only let the Grand Trunk shed its foolish Pacific extension and forget its promise to link up with the National Transcontinental, the company just might make

Postwar crowds enjoy themselves at Sunnyside beach in Toronto. After years of anxiety and sacrifice, most Canadians wanted some pleasure. Note the crowded parking lot and the seeming formality of people's clothing.

the eastern part of its system profitable. The situation called for tact and humility. Instead, the Grand Trunk declared that it was closing the Pacific line and dared the government to act. White and Meighen needed no better excuse. At once they called the government's debts and the line went officially bankrupt. On May 21, the government took over 12,805 kilometres of track, 2597 of them in the United States.

Canadian businessmen were shocked. Meighen's tough logic was not their style. The president of the Canadian Pacific Railway had offered a much pleasanter plan in their eyes. To spare Canada the horror of government ownership, the CPR would kindly take over the troubled railways, and taxpayers could pay the annual deficit. The powerful Bank of Montreal, a supporter of both the CPR and the Conservative party, backed the scheme. Meighen bluntly did not. Bad as nationalization might be in his eyes, a CPR monopoly, financed by taxpayers, was far worse.

Though Meighen had given farmers and labour the nationalized railway system they had long demanded, he got no thanks. To them, he remained the arch-conservative. In Montreal, however, Meighen became the arch-socialist, the enemy of all that the St. James Street financial community held dear. Since wealthy Montreal was the main financial base of the Conservative party, its anger would have deep consequences.

Postwar Politics

Arthur Meighen had been the driving force behind the Borden government. Always he took the harsh assignments, performing them with frigid efficiency. He had devised closure for the Naval Aid Bill of 1913. He had taken responsibility for the Military Service Act and the War-time Elections Act, deeds which neither Quebec nor the Liberals could ever forgive. No man was more associated with the postwar Union government. Meighen was strong partly because of his sheer talent, partly because so many of his colleagues were ailing, exhausted or fed up with political struggles. Meighen could command with brilliance but he could not lead. Only Borden could do that and, of all the Union ministers, few were more tired or sick of arguments. "I should be happy to return to Canada," he had written in Paris in May 1919, "were it not for politics."

Borden had come home but he had failed to keep Crerar and the farmers. Suddenly, it occurred to him, there was an alternative. In all the angry tumult of postwar Canada, there was only one area of quiet — Quebec. Bourassa was silent, fed up as well with political battles. Quebec farmers had come to Ottawa in 1918, but they had gone home again and they would not happily follow a Protestant and Conscriptionist like Crerar. Quebec labour was also split, but the new element, Catholic unionism, was fleeing from socialism, not embracing it. It was time for another meeting with Sir Lomer Gouin.

The Quebec premier was unhappy. In February 1919 the venerable Sir Wilfrid Laurier had died. The Unionists, eager to please Quebec, had ordered a costly state funeral. Gouin was pleased but he did not like the new men who ran his own party. He had placed his faith in business and the tariff, not in farmers, free trade or talk of social reform. Borden's envoy found that not only Gouin but the most eminent Quebec Liberals would be pleased to meet with the prime minister. In July, Borden set out on a holiday cruise of the St. Lawrence. At Trois Rivières, he chatted with Jacques Bureau; at Quebec he paid renewed respects to Cardinal Bégin; at Rivière-du-Loup he had tea with Ernest Lapointe. Finally, at Malbaie, the resort of Montreal's wealthy, he joined Gouin, Sir Henry Drayton and former President Taft of the United States for golf.

Borden won the game but he could not win Gouin. The Quebec premier was tempted but he knew that not even he could win as a Unionist anywhere in Quebec. Instead, Gouin waited until Liberals gathered in Ottawa for the first party leadership convention in Canadian history. Lady Laurier knew her husband's choice. Even at seventy, W. S. Fielding had experience, dignity and the power to bring back the Liberal Unionists. The young William Lyon Mackenzie King was shallow and ambitious. That was not how the delegates saw it. King was modern, an expert in the problems an industrial society would encounter. Far more important, in 1917 Fielding had betrayed Laurier; King had served him in a hopeless election struggle. Quebec delegates, mustered by Ernest Lapointe and ignoring Gouin's instructions, carried King to victory on the third ballot, 476 votes to 438.

For the Unionists, there was little more to do, but they could not bring themselves to do even that. In December, Borden's doctors insisted that he must resign or perish. It was the order he had wanted. A frightened cabinet and party caucus pleaded with him to stay. Meighen, alone, recommended that he go. The Unionists needed time to find a leader. Borden agreed to take a long vacation and return until a successor was found. Through the winter and spring of 1920 he stayed in the American south, pursued by letters and telegrams of complaint and worry. On May 12, he returned. On July 1, Dominion Day, he had had enough.

The Unionist M.P.'s wanted Meighen. Alone among the ministers, Meighen had stood up to the new Liberal leader, catching King in woolly inconsistencies, demolishing him in debate. Most ministers, more shrewdly, saw that Meighen's tactics won no converts. Borden's own choice was Sir Thomas White. The weary finance minister refused utterly. Meighen would have to be the successor. On July 10, the new prime minister took office.

The Bluenose
Canada's most famous sailing-ship, the Bluenose, was launched in early 1921. She won her first race in October and remained unbeatable through the 1920s and most of the 1930s. The likeness of the Bluenose still graces the back of the Canadian ten-cent piece.

Sir Robert Borden
After retiring, Sir Robert Borden lived on until 1937, working on his memoirs, writing and lecturing on law and external relations and observing life and politics through his private "Letters to Limbo," published long after his death.

Neckwear to Give a Modish
Air to New or Old Frocks

Including, as you will notice, the round collar that is a Special Pet of Fashion, and the little Cowl Collar that is so becoming!

Georgette Silk Collars, made in sailor style, with hemstitched edges and very pretty motifs in corners; also some pointed collars. The softness of these collars will give character and becomingness to some afternoon dress that's too dark. Price, each $2.00

The New Wash Silk Collar, trimmed with a neat frill of pleats that may easily be retained by ordinary ironing. A most useful and adaptable piece of neckwear. Each $3.15

Round Silk Collar, with pleated frill. Each $1.95

Collar and Cuff Set, of washable material, trimmed with pleated frill. A pretty set for your suit or serge dress. Each $3.15

Very New Collars of Georgette Silk, made in Cowl style. They have deep fold with a deep pleating all around $2.50

The Right Sort of Face Powder and Cream

Indispensable on every woman's dressing table.

Rigaud's Lilac Face Powder, in assorted colors, $1.25 a box.

Dorin's Rouges, in a good assortment of colors, 45c.

Seeley's Peroxide and Almond Cream, large bottles. A splendid product, 50c.

Seeley's Mahilia Face Powder, in flesh, white and brunette. A delightful toilet asset. Small size, 75c; larger size, $1.

MEAT MARKET

TUESDAY'S SPECIALS

Stewing Lamb, 2 lbs 35c

Stewing Veal, 2 lbs. 45c

Pork and Beef Sausage, 2 lbs. 35c

Hamburg Steak, 2 lbs. . 45c

Rib Boil Beef, lb. 20c

Shoulder Roast, Special, lb. 23c

Whatever The Weather May Be Today You Will Need Warm
Combinations

The excellent and dependable qualities of the following lines assure long wear and satisfaction. Considering the increased cost of wool, the prices are especially noteworthy.

—Women's Woollen Combinations, with low neck, short sleeves and ankle lengths—or V neck, long sleeves and full lengths. Prices
$2.95 $3.25 $3.49

—Women's Union Weight Vests, with V necks, short or long sleeves; also high necks. Drawers to match in ankle length. A garment 79c

—Women's Black Wool Bloomers, in knee length, finished with an elastic at waist and knee. A garment $1.35
—Main Floor.

Smallwares

"Hump" Invisible Hair Pins will not slip or fall out. Non-rust satin enamel finish, pkg. 10c.

"Hump" Hair Pins, locks the locks and are non-rust and satin enamel finish. Fine size, per pkg. 19c.

Fancy Black One-Piece Safety Pins, for blouses, etc. One dozen on card, 5c.

"Neverlost" Baby Pins, of super nickel plate. Just the thing to fasten baby's diaper and stockings. Price 20c a card.

The "Atrora" Dress Shield Pin, of heavy nickel plate; will not rust. One dozen, 5c.

SOME VERY USEFUL HOLIDAY GIFTS.

Silver Thimble and Celluloid Finger Shield, put up in a neat square plush case, 39c each.

Silver Thimble, in a neat heart and book shape plush case, each 25c.

A Pretty Box, containing 2 Silver Thimbles, 1 Celluloid Finger Shield, which will make a very useful gift, 39c.

Face Mats, 11 by 11, close weave, stitched edges. Special, 9c each.

Wash Cloths, 10" by 10" in fine Turkish weave, stitched edges. Pretty striped border in pink or blue. Each 15c.

Children's Rubber Feeders, washable, and come in neat floral patterns with neat tape bound edges. Will keep baby's dress clean and dry at meal time, each 19c.

1 Celluloid and 2 Silver Thimbles in box. Special value, 25c a box.

Wash Cloths, heavy weave and close. Some have colored border and floral pattern in centre, 2 for 35c.
—Main Floor.

A Special Group of Smart Looking
Tweed Suits
Priced for Tuesday
$20

These suits express the spirit of wartime thrift in its fullest meaning. They are made of the modish brown and grey tweeds of reliable quality, that will give plenty of service. They are fashioned in smart single-breasted style, with snug-fitting collars; the vest is medium high-cut and is lined with fine quality linings. Trousers are fashionably cut and well finished. Sizes 34 to 44. Tuesday's Price $20.00.

IT'S TIME TO PUT ON OVERCOATS.

There are large assortments here of Overcoats for conservative men, business men and younger men
$16.50 and Upwards.
—Main Floor.

GROCERIES
THE PENNIES COUNT—WATCH THEM!
Phone Queen 5040.
License No. 8-10796.

Stuart's Pure Raspberry Jam, 4 lbs. $1.09

Salmon, B.C. Pink, 30c value for 25c

California Prunes, 500 lbs only, 3 lbs. 39c

Fresh Biscuits, 2 lbs. 34c

Fresh Ground Coffee, lb. 39c

Shredded Wheat, 3 pkges. 42c

Corn Syrup, 5 lb. pails 59c

Teco Pancake Flour, 2 pkges. 38c

Corn Flakes, Krinkle, 3 pkges. 39c

Victory Breakfast Food, 5 lbs. 39c

Ground Rice or Potato Flour, 2 pkges. 25c

Shortening, 5 lbs. $1.64

Sago or Tapioca, 2 lbs. 39c

100 pkges. Cream Sodas, pkge. 15c

Fresh Rolled Oats, 7 lbs. 55c

Strawberry-Apple Jelly, bottle 35c

Rice, good quality, 2 lbs. 24c

Canadian Boiled Dinner, can . 25c

Maple Sugar, cake 10c

Carrots, per gal. 15c

Red Onions, 6 lbs. 25c

Spaghetti, already prepared, can .... 20c and 25c

Clark's Tomato Catsup, bottle .... 25c and 40c

Clark's Pork and Beans, 2 cans 39c

Veal, Ham and Tongue Pate, can 25c

Heinz's Pork and Beans, can .. 25c

Chili Sauce, bottle 35c

Butter Cream Sodas, pkge. 29c

LAUNDRY SPECIALS.

Cosmos Laundry Soap, 10 bars 65c

Laundry Starch, 3 lbs. 38c

Powdered Ammonia, 2 pkges. .. 23c

Hand Cleaner, 3 cans 29c

Gold Dust, large pkges. 29c

98c
Buys 2 Saucepans
1 six quart and 1 four quart of Well known
McCLARY'S ENAMELWARE
Regular Price of the 2 is $1.60
While They last 98c
—Main Floor.

Now is the Best Time for a Woman to Buy Her Winter
COAT
We Will Feature on Tuesday Three Special Groups at
$35, $37.50 and $45

An inspection of these Coats in our Women's Ready-to-Wear Department, on the Second Floor, will reveal their exceptional beauty and their moderateness in price.

EVERY COAT IN THESE GROUPS WAS ORDERED TO THESE SPECIFICATIONS.

FABRICS—fine woollens, heavy in texture and light in weight, including rough weaves as well as the smooth fineness of Velours.

STYLES—the smartest of the season, embodying every new whim of Fashion.

WORKMANSHIP—quite as carefully executed as in Coats priced much higher than these.

The sleeves—the skirts—front lacings—buttonholes — linings — seams — are care finished in every detail. These may seem little things of themselves, but their sum means EXTRA WEAR TO EVERY COAT BOUGHT HERE.
—Second Floor.

In 1919, at the age of seventeen, Elsie Freeman found a job in a garment factory. Once she became a skilled seamstress, she earned $10 a week. She paid $2.50 a week rent for a furnished room. Based on the prices shown in these ads, estimate the probable cost of other necessities and make up a budget for Elsie.

An unskilled male worker earned about the same as Elsie. Do you think he and his family could afford the kind of holiday pictured in the ad on the opposite page?

Little now remained, even of the Unionists. Meighen restored the old party name of Conservative and set out to bring back those who had scorned the coalition. There was only one small hope of victory: it was to run again on the issue of 1911. By the autumn of 1921, a year of office had done nothing for the fortunes of his party. Liberals in Quebec and farmers in the West swept every by-election. The worst of the postwar depression was over, but grim memories count more than hopes when people judge a government. The Unionist majority of seventy-one in 1917 was now only twenty-one. On September 1, Meighen announced an election for December 1.

The campaign would be fought in Ontario and the West. Quebec was doubly hopeless. In rural ridings, rumours ran that if Meighen won, Orangemen would "pilfer the consecrated wafers in the churches and feed them to the pigs they lead in the streets." A Montreal, newspaper claimed that Meighen would move the Grand Trunk headquarters and 50,000 jobs from the city to Toronto. Conservative fundraisers came back from Montreal ears ringing and empty-handed. Meighen, alone among the leaders, braved Quebec audiences, but he spent his time fighting for the tariff.

In 1911, the target had been clear enough: a reciprocity agreement signed and almost delivered. King offered no such target. The Liberal convention's promises were, he said, "a chart." Liberals believed in a revenue tariff that would protect farmers, manufacturers and people of all classes but not multi-millionaires, monopolies and trusts. Meighen described King's policy as "Protection on apples in British Columbia, Free Trade on the Prairie Provinces and the rural parts of Ontario, protection in industrial centres in Ontario, no Conscription in Quebec and humbug in the Maritime Provinces."

It was a fair description of King's tactics and it made no difference at all. On election day, the Liberals took every seat in Quebec and a scattering in Ontario and the Maritimes to emerge with a national total of 117. Crerar's Progressives swept the West and much of rural Ontario to come second, with 65. Meighen's party won seats in only three provinces, New Brunswick, Ontario and British Columbia, to hold at total of 50. North Winnipeg gave J. S. Woodsworth a close victory over a Communist, Jake Penner. Calgary confirmed its radical reputation by sending a second labour member to Parliament.

In 1911, Canadians had chosen a national government, with support in every region of the country. A decade later, a new election showed only how deep the divisions had since gone. Under Borden, Canadians had done great things but they had not done them together. A national leader of integrity and humane convictions had divided his country as no politician had done before. The divisions were not simply those of French and English but of worker and employer, country and city, East and West.

The divisions of Canada in 1921 would heal. Canadians would, in time, recognize the growth in status which wartime sacrifices and postwar diplomacy had brought them. The war years had hurled a semi-rural Canada into a modern world in which governments had to be efficient and honest, in which women finally enjoyed economic and human rights, in which the provision of jobs and incomes could no longer be left to the hidden hand of economic forces.

Canada was not modern yet. The war was over. Canadians would seek for a time to return to those *Sunshine Sketches of a Little Town* with which we began. They would never find them because they had always been fiction.

REVIEW AND DISCUSSION

Key People and Ideas
Explain the importance of each of the following people and ideas as they are discussed in the chapter.

Gideon Robertson	Article X of the League of Nations Treaty
Bob Russell	The One Big Union
Henry Wise Wood	The Trades and Labour Congress
Ernest Drury	The "New National Policy"
W. L. Mackenzie King	

Analysing the Issues
Answer each of the following questions, which deal with important issues raised in the chapter.
— What events led Canada to have an independent seat at the Paris Peace Conference and in the League of Nations?
— What factors led to the economic depression of 1919 in Canada?
— What factors led to the Winnipeg General Strike of 1919?
— What problems were faced by veterans when they returned home in 1919?
— What factors led to the Liberal victory in the election of 1921?

Questions for Discussion
Think carefully about each of the following questions and discuss the issues they raise.
— J. W. Dafoe declared of the prime minister in the postwar period that "it is going to be demanded of him that he do things which cannot be done; things which are mutually contradictory and destructive, and whatever he does will have more critics than friends." Was the defeat of the Borden/Meighen government inevitable given the social and economic turmoil which followed the war? What different directions might the government have taken in these difficult years?

Further Reading

There are many books and articles on this period in Canadian history and more are being published all the time. Here are some samples, to help you to find more information or other ideas. Remember that no historian knows the whole story.

- Armstrong, Elizabeth. *The Crisis of Quebec, 1914-1918.* Toronto: McClelland & Stewart, 1974. A useful analysis, first published in 1937, of Quebec's reaction to Canada's participation in the war and to the introduction of conscription in 1917.
- Bercuson, David. *Fools and Wise Men: The Rise and Fall of the One Big Union.* Toronto: McGraw-Hill Ryerson, 1978. An excellent book on labour radicalism during and after the war.
- Bercuson, David and McNaught, Kenneth. *The Winnipeg Strike, 1919.* Don Mills: Longman's, 1974. A short but balanced account of a major postwar event.
- Berger, Carl. *Conscription, 1917.* Toronto: University of Toronto Press, 1969. A collection of articles on all aspects of the conscription question.
- Bird, W. R. *Ghosts Have Warm Hands.* Toronto: Clarke Irwin, 1976. One of the best accounts by any participant in the war of what the fighting was like for individual soldiers.
- Bliss, Michael. *A Canadian Millionaire: The Life and Business Times of Sir Joseph Flavelle, 1858-1939.* Toronto: Macmillan, 1978. This biography of the head of the Imperial Munitions Board provides a good look at Canada's munitions industry.
- Brown, R. Craig and Cook, Ramsay. *Canada 1896-1921: A Nation Transformed.* A carefully balanced account of twenty-five eventful years.
- Craig, John. *The Years of Agony.* Toronto: McClelland and Stewart, 1977. This profusely illustrated book provides a wealth of fascinating information on Canadian life between 1910 and 1920.
- English, John. *Borden: His Life and World.* Toronto: McGraw-Hill Ryerson, 1977. A general yet detailed survey of the social, political and economic realities of Canada from the turn of the century to 1921.
- Goodspeed, D. J. *The Road Past Vimy: The Canadian Corps, 1914-1918.* Toronto: Macmillan, 1969. A short, readable analysis of Canadian military operations in the first World War.
- Leacock, Stephen. *Arcadian Adventures with the Idle Rich* and *Sunshine Sketches of a Little Town.* Toronto: McClelland and Stewart (New Canadian Library) 1959, 1960. These two books by Canada's best-known humorist tell us a lot about what life was like in prewar Canada.
- McClung, Nellie. *In Times Like These.* Toronto: University of Toronto Press, 1972. The famous suffragist's writings, first published in 1915, provide a valuable insight into the times.
- Morton, Desmond. *A Peculiar Kind of Politics.* Toronto: University of Toronto Press, 1982. A view of Canada's growth to self-government during the war years.
- Read, Daphne (ed.). *The Great War and Canadian Society: An Oral History.* Toronto: New Hogtown Press, 1978. This book provides interesting insights into how the war affected Canadians, but the reader must remember that it is based on people's memories over half a century — not always the most accurate evidence.
- Swettenham, John. *Canada and the First World War.* Toronto: McGraw-Hill, 1973. A solid, clearly written account of the services of the Canadian Corps overseas.
- Wise, S. F. *Canadian Airmen and the First World War.* Toronto: University of Toronto Press, 1980. A recent, very detailed history of the newest dimension of war.

Index